*UNTANGLING
LIFE'S CORE ISSUES*

KNOT

by

KNOT

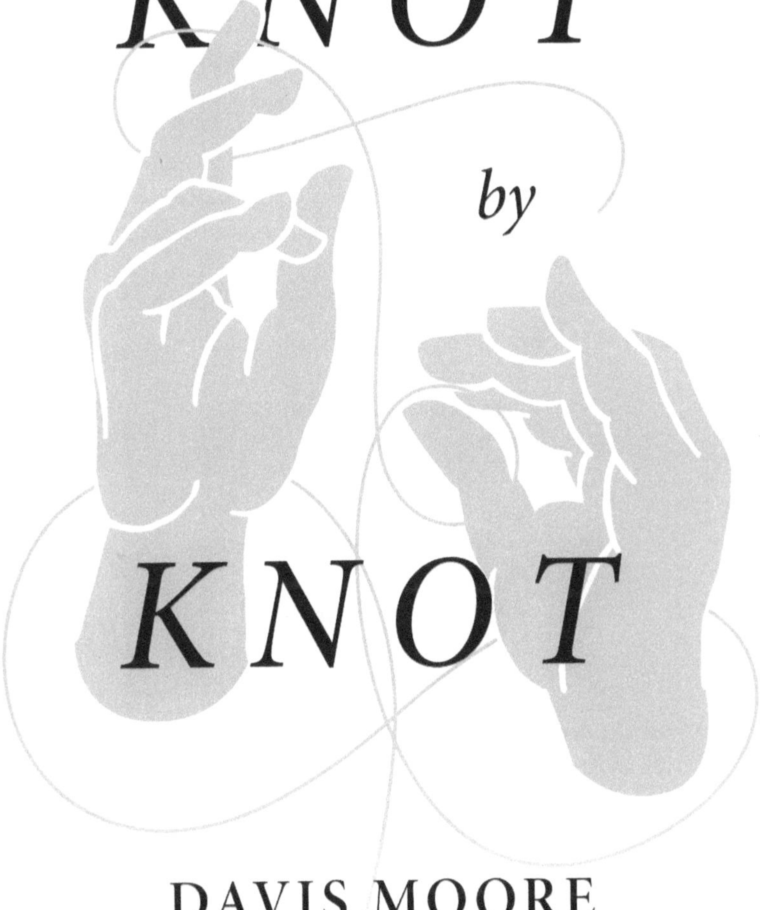

DAVIS MOORE

Published by Humble Books

www.davismooreauthor.com

Scripture quotations, unless otherwise noted, are from The Holy
Bible, English Standard Version, copyright © 2001 by Crossway
Bibles, a division of Good News Publishers. Used by permission.

Jacket Design: Christian Rafetto

Book Design: Christian Rafetto

ISBN 13 TP: 979-8-9905028-0-2

ISBN 13 eBook: 979-8-9905028-1-9

For Worldwide Distribution

Humble Books is a company of Jesus-followers, who are passionate about publishing books that build the Kingdom, and doing so
in a way that honors God and blesses our authors and readers.

Find out more about us at

www.humblebooksmedia.com

To my wife who has my whole heart.

Free Study Guide

Follow the QR code to download
the free study guide for *Knot by Knot*.

C O N T E N T S

PART ONE

UNTANGLING KNOTS

THE GRAVEYARD RUNNER

I love to run in graveyards. There is something cathartic about watching headstone after headstone pass in my peripheral while I run. Before long, I began to recognize a pattern to the gravestones. Some were small, resting against the grass, like pillows. Others were large, six-foot pillars with deep-cut letters that could be read from a hundred yards. Some were new, as evidenced by a recent date etched in stone; others were old and unreadable, attracting moss blankets. Yet, whether fancy or simple, each stone marked a human husk returning to dust.

As I run, I cannot help but wonder if they lived life well; if the dash between birth and death could tell a story not only lived for happiness and pleasure but for a grander purpose. I wonder if their days passed numbly with silent, unheard heartbreaks or if they were lived powerfully. Some of the headstones mark lives which were long-lived, lives which surely saw grandchildren or great-grandchildren. Others revealed they perished in adolescence or had never even seen a first birthday.

We often forget we are not promised tomorrow. Most of us do not pass at a time that we expect. Most people leave unfinished house projects, unspent fortunes, missed vacations, and family holiday parties behind.

Running through graveyards reminds me of my transience. In our society, we worship our attempts at immortality. We build our walls of cash and 401k, workout regimens, and consumerism like barriers around us, numbing ourselves to the reality of our existence. The truth is no matter how wealthy we are, how much we hustle, work, pursue pleasure, or enjoy life, we will one day rest here six feet underground, marked by varying sizes of headstones. All our striving and energy one day returns to dust.

This finality of life sometimes hollows me. Funerals remind us of the fact one day all of us are going to vacate these mortal bodies. I remember, several years ago, watching my grandma be buried. The casket was lowered by a machine into a rectangular hole. Its descent felt like an eternity as a million memories flashed behind my eyes. My grandmother was the embodiment of life. As a child, I remember scents of apple or blueberry pies wafting through the house as she baked in the kitchen. She was always cooking or baking some delicious new recipe. In the evenings, she sat in her chair with the tangle of strings and pins of her latest sewing project while she watched soap operas with my grandfather. Most of all, as the casket descended, I could hear her laugh. She had an infectious laugh, which often lingered on the air, reverberating off our eardrums long after its physical sound ceased.

We often try to suppress the fact that the moments we live in are temporary. We inoculate and numb ourselves with social media and cheap thrills—giving ourselves the façade that our life is evergreen. We fill our days with podcasts, movies, and online content; we avoid the moments of quiet because they cause us to reflect. Nonetheless, no matter how much we push or pull, one day we all are carried in a box by six men in suits and laid into a hole in the ground. Our stories end here.

Sometimes, when I run in graveyards, I wonder what motivated them in life. What were those things which got them out of bed in the morning? What motivated their actions and propelled them to chase dreams or do the right thing? Sometimes I wonder what motivates my actions. What motivates me to be the man I am? What pushes me to be man I wish to be?

I think most of us can say we wish we were better. We wish we did not yell at the kids as much. Or we did not tremble with anxiety. Or maybe we could break our pornography addiction. And many of us, at one time or another, have willed ourselves to not struggle with such things anymore, resolving next time, when the trigger came up, we would not give in. And our resolutions may even work for a short time, but our vices have a way of tricking us into thinking they have loosened their grip before they return with a serpentine chokehold around our throat.

We often view our issues as skin-deep. In fact, there are entire genres of books marketed to overcome our issues. A lot of these manuals are usually titled something like *5 Steps to Overcome YOUR Bad Habits* or *How to be a Better YOU!* And usually on the front cover there is a picture of the smiling author standing with one foot atop a chair with a set of teeth too white to be natural. These books focus on ways to change people's behaviors but often fail to get to the root of why the issues are present in the first place.

The problem is most of our issues are not skin-deep. Most of our vices are not as simple as *5 Steps to Living Your Best Life.* Many of our issues have a taproot, which drives deep within us, knotted and balled up, tangling around our bones and ligaments.

As a pastor, I have talked with many individuals who have told me they would never be free from the issues which haunted them. I had one man who wrestled with anger tell me, dejectedly, "I wouldn't know who I would be without my anger." Another woman said she could not picture her marriage fixed. Another man felt like he could never feel valued, truly valued, by other people.

The truth is, all of us face these systemic issues, which feel so knotted and tied to who we are. And maybe most of us believe these issues are the things we are going to take to the grave. We believe freedom is not an option, and our issues are terminal.

When Christ came to earth, He spoke about the burdens we bear. He said, "Come to me, all who labor and are heavy laden, and I will give you rest. Take my yoke upon you, and learn from me, for I am gentle and lowly in heart, and you will find rest for your souls. For my yoke is easy, and my burden is light" (Matthew 11:28-30). Jesus is not only talking to the people who are struggling with minor issues or who come from a good home. He is talking to the drug addicts. He is talking to the people who feel the need to impress everyone around them or who feel like they are always going to be a burden to others. He is looking at the people in the crowd who boil with anger and lust. He is talking to everyone.

Christ did not come to set up a cold set of religious systems for people to follow so they could change their behavior. He came to free all of us from our deepest, knotted issues. Those issues which have us in bondage, tied up so tight we believe escape is impossible.

So many Christians today believe all God wants out of them is a signature agreeing to a doctrinal statement and a consistent seat at church on Sunday mornings. But God is not just calling us to a good theology or church attendance; He is calling us out of death and into a new life.

When we embrace the gospel of Jesus, it should change us. Embracing the gospel is not taking a bunch of rules and combining them with our other beliefs. It is a surrender of who we are and picking up God's identity for us. Many people think of Christianity as a set of rules to change our outward behavior. God is not looking for people who just know the Bible or are simply nice to other people. He is looking for a new creation. In his book *Mere Christianity*, C.S. Lewis talks about this new creation:

> *A world of nice people, content with their own niceness, looking no further, turned away from God, would be just as desperately in need of salvation as a miserable world—and might be more difficult to save. For mere improvement is not redemption, though redemption will always improve people even here and now and will, in the end, improve them to a degree we cannot yet imagine. God became man*

to turn creatures into sons: not simply to produce better men of the old kind but to produce a new kind of man.[1]

God is not after some behavioral modification that makes people nice to have around. That is not redemption. That is just behavioral improvement. God is calling us to so much more. He is calling us to a change of identity—an identity deeper than just a piece of our heart; God is after the entire thing. This does not mean, however, that as soon as someone becomes a believer in Jesus, that they magically transform into a perfect person who is committed to participating in God's story. Growing to be like Jesus is a lifelong process.

That is what this book is about. How do we overcome the deepest issues in our lives? How do we truly change so deeply our behavior is the outcome, not the goal? What does it look like for us to step into the process of change?

In the first half of the book, we are going to look at a theology of change. We will learn how we step into the process of change and grow in our relationship with Christ.

In the second half of the book, we will dive deep into some of life's core issues and how to walk through them and experience victory.

The truth is, we do not have to take our issues to the grave. You do not have to sit in bondage. There was a Savior who already took those things to the tomb with Him. You can experience freedom because He did not stay dead. Not only did He take those sins to the grave, when He rose from the dead, He rose victorious over sin and death. It is in the power of Jesus' victory over sin and death that we too can have victory, untangling our deepest issues, knot by knot.

A COUNTED COST

If we are going to talk about how to overcome our core issues, we must start at the beginning. Before we start the process of change, we must know the cost of it. We need to start with the gospel.

The truth is, as the Church in the United States, we have corrupted the gospel. In many ways, we treat it like life insurance. It does not do you much good now, but later you will be thankful for it after something happens to your earthly body.

I used to think the gospel and salvation were about avoiding going to hell. In fact, when I first accepted Christ, I was four years old. I was terrified of going to hell, and I begged my mom to lead me through the prayer so I would not have to go there. I know I am not the only one who once thought that. I was raised in the conservative church, where presentations of the gospel were always focused on getting to heaven rather than a lake of burning fire for all eternity. I remember the presentations of hell being much more vivid than the presentations of paradise. Occasionally someone would respond positively to the gospel that way, and I would wonder how many times people were just like four-year-old me, not wanting to suffer.

I once was at an all-night event for youth groups. It was a high-octane event, including a hockey game, bowling, inflatable obstacle courses, pizza, and games at a nearby university recreational center. About 1,500 teenagers attend this event year after year. Immediately after the hockey game, there was typically a presentation of the gospel. It was a strange moment in the night, where all the yelling and commotion quieted for about fifteen minutes and a thousand pairs of eyes locked on a solitary man speaking from the ice. It was the gospel message, and he spoke about a God who loved us so much that He died for us so we could go to heaven someday.

After the message was over, my wife, Amanda, came up to me and asked, "Did anything about that message feel off to you?"

"What do you mean?" I asked.

"Well, he didn't talk about the cost of salvation. Sure, it's a free gift. But we have to die," she responded.

Those words stuck with me that night because she was right. The idea of death and resurrection are intrinsically tied together in the gospel. And not only in the physical death, burial, and resurrection of Jesus but also in the spiritual death of our old lives as well. In many parts of our evangelical circles today, we talk about heaven as this destination we go to someday. Many Christians talk about praying a prayer so we can be forgiven so we can go to heaven when we die.

However, the main purpose of the gospel is not glorified life insurance. Its main purpose is not praying a prayer to go to heaven someday. It is not a grand retirement plan, "better than the alternative" of eternal judgment. This type of Christianity creates disciples who are more concerned about punching their ticket to heaven than actually growing into the image of Jesus. Jesus was not just after changing our destinations; He wants to change us—every last piece of us. A failure to understand the true purpose of the gospel is to miss the entire thing.

I once knew a church in Michigan who claimed to reach their entire town for the cause of Christ. They bragged they had gone door to door to every house in town and every person in every home had claimed Christ as their Savior or prayed with the church's representatives to ask Jesus into their heart. The church was ecstatic about this realization. They felt that they had reached their entire town and had completed the Great Commission in their immediate sphere of influence. While I am sure this crusade started with the greatest intentions, it is not a true embrace of the Great Commission in daily life as Christ intended. The church was able to convince people heaven would be good and hell was bad, but the true cost of salvation was missed.

The gospel may be free, but it costs us everything. In Luke chapter 14, Jesus talked about this cost.

> *"If anyone comes to me and does not hate his own father and mother and wife and children and brothers and sisters, yes, even his own life, he cannot be my disciple. Whoever does not bear his own cross and come after me cannot be my disciple." (Luke 14:25-27)*

Jesus made a radical claim here. He said in order to be His disciples, we have to hate those closest to us and even our own lives. Jesus was not saying you can no longer go to Thanksgiving because you are commanded to be angry with your parents. God created the family to be loved and cherished. There are many places in Scripture which talk about the importance of family, taking care of family, and supporting the family unit. Instead, what He is getting at is our love for God should be so all-consuming and devoted, there should be nothing which comes even close to that level of affection in our lives. Our devotion in life and death is tied completely and totally to Christ.

He also says, "Whoever does not bear his own cross and come after me cannot be my disciple" (Luke 14:27). I think we often miss the language being used here. In our current culture, we wear silver crosses around our neck or have a porcelain cross hanging on the wall in our living room with a verse scribbled across it. To us, it is a pretty decoration. We like the idea of picking up a pretty thing we could pose with for our social media accounts.

Many of us look back on the cross as a redemptive instrument that fills us with emotion when we look at it. By no means is this a wrong emotion. We should be able to look at the cross and be filled with a heart of gratitude longing to be joined to its Savior. However, the connotation of the word "cross" in Jesus' day was much different. To the hearers gathered around Jesus, it was an execution device—a horrible, painful, dirty, shameful execution device. Only nefarious criminals were put on crosses. It would be like Jesus saying to us today, "Pick up your electric chair and follow me." That is a much different connotation than wearing a trendy necklace. Jesus was calling them to die. Calling them to join Him in His walk to death.

For some of the people present, He was speaking of a physical death. Most of the disciples who were standing with Him also died as martyrs for their faith in Christ. But Jesus here was also talking of another type of death. He was talking of the death of the self. This type of death reveals itself in several different ways.

The first aspect of the death of self is one where we realize and accept the truth that we bring nothing that makes us worthy of God's love. None of our good works, charm, work ethic, or financial stability can make us more worthy of God's love and forgiveness. This is an acceptance of what Scripture clearly says: "For all have sinned and fallen short of the glory of God" (Romans 3:23). Our ego and attempts at self-sufficiency must be put to the side.

The second component of the death of self is the surrender of our will, which claims control over the direction of our lives, insists on its own way, and holds its life like a closed fist. Disciples of Jesus lay down their own wills to pick up Christ's will as the compass for their lives. The death of self means we recognize we bring nothing to salvation but our sin.

This was not the first time in the book of Luke Jesus had talked like this. In Luke 9, He said something similar, yet with an added word. "If anyone would come after me, let him deny himself and take up his cross daily and follow me. For whoever would save his life will lose it, but whoever loses his life for my sake will save it" (Luke 9:23-24). Daily pick up your cross. Following Christ is not a one-time walk down the aisle altar call decision to keep us from going to hell when we die. Following Jesus is a daily decision of dying. Dietrich Bonhoeffer, a German pastor who lived, ministered, and was martyred during Hitler's Nazi regime, once said, "When Christ calls a man, He bids him come and die."[2] While not all of us will be crucified or martyred for our faith in a physical death, we are all called to die to our own wills, desires, and plans every single day for the kingdom of God.

The Apostle Paul had an understanding of this. He once said, "I have been crucified with Christ. It is no longer I who live, but Christ who lives in me. And the life I now live in the flesh I live by faith in the Son of God, who loved me and gave himself for me" (Galatians 2:20). Paul, at the core of his being, realized that his commitment to Christ necessitated a death of himself. Before his conversion to Christianity, Paul—then Saul—had climbed to a high rank in Judaism. He was a religious prodigy of sorts who was zealous for his beliefs and was going places. In fact, he was gaining major recognition because he was passionately killing and throwing Christians in jail.

However, on his way to persecute more Christians, Saul was met by Christ on the road to Damascus. Rather than smiting Saul for his violent actions against Christians, God beckoned the man to follow Him. Saul's life was utterly transformed by this encounter. He could no longer be Saul the persecutor, who killed Christians. He could no longer be Saul the religious prodigy. He could no longer be the young preacher the culture was looking forward to see rising to prominence. Saul, in a moment, realized his entire old identity, his way of marking himself for who he was, needed to change.

This event is what led Paul to say in Galatians, "I am crucified with Christ." That is to say, "My old self which I used to define who I was and the old self which gave me value in this life, that man is dead." To follow Jesus means to say it is no longer our story and ambitions driving us. Instead, we submit to pick up the ambition and story which Christ is sharing in us. When we come to Christ, it is not only a saying sorry for the bad stuff we have done in the past; it is laying down our entire being and saying to Christ, "It is Yours."

That is why when Jesus presented the gospel to the rich young ruler, the man found it hard to accept.

> *And as he was setting out on his journey, a man ran up and knelt before him and asked him, "Good Teacher, what must I do to inherit eternal life?" And Jesus said to him, "Why do you call me good? No one is good except God alone. You know the commandments: 'Do not murder, Do not commit adultery, Do not steal, Do not bear false witness, Do not defraud, Honor your father and mother.'" And he said to him, "Teacher, all these I have kept from my youth." And Jesus, looking at him, loved him, and said to him, "You lack one thing: go, sell all that you have and give to the poor and you will*

have treasure in heaven: and come, follow me." Dis-
heartened by the saying, he went away sorrowful,
for he had great possessions. (Mark 10:18-22)

This young, rich man came and asked Jesus a pret-ty simple question: How do I know for sure I am going to heaven? Personally, I have heard plenty of Baptist sermons start out with this very question before the preacher goes on to explain the gospel. This is one of those golden opportunities for Jesus. He could have easily done this. He had a guy who was ready to pray the prayer and ask Jesus into his heart. It would have even been a financially smart decision for Jesus to have this young, rich man funding his campaign all the way to Jerusalem. But Jesus did something dif-ferent here. He began instead by talking about all the commandments the man should obey.

I believe He did this because the young man was looking for something tangible he could do, and Je-sus needed to show him entering into eternal life was more than only doing the right things. When the young man said he had kept all the law from his youth, Jesus agreed. I can almost see the desperation in the young man's eyes, as he looked down at his hands and con-sidered all the effort he had expended on keeping the law, while he waited for Jesus' next instruction. Jesus said, "One thing you lack, go sell all you have and give to the poor and you will have treasure in heaven: and come, follow me" (Mark 10:21).

This statement was striking for the rich man. It was a blade cutting to his heart, between flesh and spirit. The text goes on to say he walked away from Jesus sorrowful, because he had spent his life acquiring much wealth. Jesus here is not saying being rich is wrong, or in order to follow Jesus we must become financially poor. He was confronting the heart of a young man who boasted about being very religious and zealous for his faith, when in actuality his heart and identity were consumed with his wealth. Deep down, the man loved his money and the comfort his wealth brought him more than the life that springs from a relationship with the Father. We do not know the end of the story for this young man, but the text tells us he walked away from Jesus, back to the comfort he loved.

With this story, Jesus is saying salvation is more than punching a ticket to heaven and more than praying a prayer. It is a reorientation of life itself. There is an interesting line in the text we often overlook. When Jesus tells the man to go and sell all he has, He adds something. He says, "to go and give it to the poor." I do not know this man's heart or attitude, but could it be that this young man looked down on the poor? Could it be when he was leaving Costco and saw the man in raggedy clothes at the stoplight holding a sign which said, "Anything helps," with a Folgers coffee tin resting at his feet, he would scoff and think any money the man would get would end up going to buy drugs or alcohol? Or maybe he judgmentally thought they would not be in this predicament if they would just get up and get a job. Did this man view himself as better than the poor? The gospel not only confronts the sin in our hearts, it also radically changes how we view people. Jesus was after this man's affections and heart, not just his belief system.

Jesus' mission was deeper than only changing our eternal destinations. He came to change the very nature of people. He came to unwind the curse of sin founded in the Garden of Eden when Adam and Eve sinned against God. He came to melt our prejudices against other people and to untie the knots of our generational curses. He walked to the hill of Golgotha so we may experience freedom from our sin and vices.

The gospel itself changes the very nature of our identity. It is not a password that makes the bouncer outside of heaven let you in the kingdom. It is the very lifeblood that changes who we are away from who we were. J.D. Greear once said, "The gospel is not the diving board from which we dive into the pool of Christianity, it is the pool itself."[3] Our experience with salvation is not launched by the gospel into the deeper truths of spirituality; it is the entire experience. For while there are many theological views and doctrines, all of them find their root in the gospel. A true experience with Christ through the gospel changes the motivation for our lives and supersedes our religiosity. It changes the way we interact with ourselves and the way we interact with others. It is a holistic transformation, and it cannot be compartmentalized into only some areas of our lives.

To experience the gospel is to be changed. There is no way around it. The gospel is free, but it costs us everything. The cost of the new nature is the death of the old. The first step in lasting change, in the killing of our old identity, is counting the cost to pick up our cross and follow after Christ.

ALREADY, NOT YET

Not too long ago, our church ran a sermon series called "Asking for a Friend." In the series, we took congregation submitted questions and answered them as a panel during our Sunday morning service. Everyone loved it. For weeks before our series started, we had dozens of questions pour in to be answered. We received many great inquiries. Some questions were theological like, "How does predestination work?" While others were deeply personal, like, "Why does God let us have incurable diseases?"

One of the questions we received was, "Why do we need to keep asking forgiveness for our sin, if God has already forgiven us?" It was a great question. I think it highlights what oftentimes is a blind spot in our theology. What actually happens to us at salvation? In our last chapter we talked about the steep cost of following Christ. But what actually happens when we count the cost of following after Christ? What changes in us?

And to answer that question, we must understand the difference between Positional and Practical Righteousness.

In the book of Ephesians, the Apostle Paul shared about the change the gospel makes. He spent the first fifteen verses of the chapter laying out the breathtaking nature of the gospel. He wrote,

> *Paul, an apostle of Christ Jesus, by the will of God. To all the saints who are in Ephesus, and are faithful in Christ Jesus: Grace to you and peace from God our Father and the Lord Jesus Christ. Blessed be the God and Father of our Lord Jesus Christ, who has blessed us in Christ with every spiritual blessing in the heavenly places, even as he chose us in Him before the foundation of the world, that we should be holy and blameless before Him. In love He predestined us for adoption to Himself as sons through Jesus Christ, according to the purpose of His will, to the praise of His glorious Grace, with which He has blessed us in the Beloved. (Ephesians 1:1-6)*

Paul started by introducing himself. He gave an inaugural blessing to the Church as he opened the letter. Then he dove right into the identity changing nature of the gospel by saying we were chosen and predestined to be sons and called holy and blameless before God. I know there are many interpretations about whether God chose us based on our future faith or just His divine choosing, which is a debate we will not enter into here. Regardless, the beauty of the gospel remains.

Paul continues his thought: "In Him, we have redemption through His blood, the forgiveness of our trespasses, according to the riches of His grace, which He lavished upon us in all wisdom and insight" (Ephesians 1:7-8). I love that word "lavished." When I was young, my brother and I used to go to waterparks with my grandparents. One of my favorite parts was going to a playground that had streams of water shooting everywhere. There were slides and guns and cannons which would shoot water, and tubes sprayed water all over the park; it was impossible to leave the playground without being completely drenched. However, my favorite part was in the center of the playground. There was a giant bucket suspended about twenty feet into the air which filled slowly, and about every ten minutes, water would dump all over the playground. Kids would rush from all over the playground to stand in the splash zone and be completely drenched by the deluge. I remember standing directly underneath it, overwhelmed by the sound of the rushing water and the pressure against my body as the torrent flowed all over me. That is what I picture when I see the word "lavished": completely drenched and covered. That is the amount of grace and forgiveness we have been given through the gospel. And it does not take ten minutes to refill; it never stops pouring.

That is the inheritance we have come to in Christ. It is not just a creed to be believed, or an adoption which allows us access to heaven someday. It is the complete and total forgiveness of our sin and a continued, eternal lavished shower of grace we have been given. When that realization hits our bones, it changes us. It pushes us past a religious duty to go to church and read the Bible. It is a call beckoning us into a pursuit of a living God.

Some attribute a French poet by the name of Antoine de Saint-Exupéry for saying, "If you want to build a ship, don't drum up the men to gather wood, divide the work, and give orders. Instead, teach them to yearn for the vast and endless sea." The same can be said of God. In our salvation, He is not only giving us a manual and a pile of wood to assemble the gospel, go to church, and sing a bunch of songs; but He, through salvation, is also beckoning and teaching us to yearn for the endless ocean called God.

When you entered into a relationship with Christ, your identity changed. You were given what theologians call "Positional Righteousness" before God. Meaning, upon receiving salvation, you were completely, wholly, utterly, forgiven. 1 Peter 3:18 says, "For Christ suffered once for sin, the righteous for the unrighteous, that he might bring us to God, being put to death in the flesh but made alive in the spirit." Peter says Christ suffered once for sin in order to bring us back to God.

This revelation would have been mind-blowing for many of the Jewish people of the time who were used to living under the Old Covenant religious system. The Jewish people were used to growing bulls and goats from infancy only to watch the animals' throats get slashed and watch the blood pour over the altar for their personal sin over and over, year after year, until they themselves died. Their children, and their children's children, would do it over and over again as well. The book of Hebrews continues this thought:

> *Day after day, every priest stands and performs his religious duties; again and again he offers the same sacrifices, which can never take away sins. But when this priest [Jesus] had offered for all time one sacrifice for sins, he sat down at the right hand of God, and since that time he waits for his enemies*

> *to be made his footstool. For by one sacrifice he has*
> *made perfect for ever those who are being made*
> *holy. (Hebrews 10:11-14)*

The writer is showing how the cross is different from the sacrificial system. No longer, in order to maintain a right standing with God, did one have to continually go to a priest and sacrifice bulls and goats. Through the sacrifice of Christ on the cross, He brought us near to God. In one sacrifice, Christ took all of the sins of mankind on Himself. Your past sins, your present sins, and the sins you will do in the future you have not even begun to think of yet. They were all put on Christ in one moment.

At the cross, something happened which theologians call "The Great Transfer." Not only did Jesus take all of your sin on Himself, but, in salvation, Christ transferred to you His righteousness, His perfect, spotless standing before God. So when you stand before God, He no longer sees addict, adulterer, liar, or chronically anxious. Instead, He sees His Son. He sees His own child.

This is why Paul, in Ephesians 1, says we can be "lavished" by the riches of God's grace. Not because we have done anything to earn it, but because of what Christ did for us. That is also how Ephesians 1 says we can be holy and blameless before God. That is positional righteousness. In salvation, because of Christ, we stand positionally holy before Him. Our identity, according to Christ's righteousness, *is* holy. At salvation, we are given a positional righteousness, making us holy before God.

With this concept in mind, we must turn to the idea of practical righteousness. For while positional righteousness makes us positionally holy before God, I think we can all say, oftentimes, our practical lives fall far short of holiness. We slip back into old habits, return to our vices we hate and love all at the same time.

When we enter into a relationship with Christ, we enter into a process called "sanctification." A process by which, moment by moment, hour by hour, setback by setback, our identity and life is transformed to be like Christ.

We see this tension in our Hebrews passage we read earlier:

> *But when this priest [Jesus] had offered for all time one sacrifice for sins, he sat down at the right hand of God, and since that time he waits for his enemies to be made his footstool. For by one sacrifice he has made perfect forever those who are being made holy. (Hebrews 10:12-14)*

"For by one sacrifice he has *made perfect* forever those who are *being made holy*." Do you see the tension communicated in this verse? There is a past tense "made perfect" at salvation, and a present progressive tense in "those who are being made holy." There is a sense of already and not yet. We are positionally covered, holy, and forgiven. And the process of learning and growing and changing is sanctification. That is practical righteousness. Or as another pastor named Stuart Briscoe has said, "Sanctification is learning to become what you became." You are learning to become holy, as you became holy at the cross.

Sanctification goes beyond moralism. This is not behavior modification or "trying to be a better person." This is the carving of the soul to follow after the image of its Creator. It is a process of walking in a new identity, while continually dying to ourselves and our natural inclinations.

Practical righteousness is a painful, lifelong process which demands all from us, but it is a work to which Christ is totally committed to complete. Paul says this in his letter to the Philippians, "I am sure of this, that he who began a good work in you will bring it to completion at the day of Jesus Christ" (1:6). Christ's mission was not only to make you positionally holy, but to reorient and align your life and heart to the Father. And He will not rest until that work is completed. C.S. Lewis, in his book *Mere Christianity*, talks about this:

> *Whatever suffering it may cost you in your earth life, whatever inconceivable purification it may cost you after death, whatever it costs Me, I will never rest, nor let you rest, until you are literally perfect—*

until my Father can say without reservation that
He is well pleased with you, as He said He was well
pleased with me. This I can do and will do. But I
will not do anything less.[4]

"I will never rest, nor let you rest, until you are liter-
ally perfect—until my Father can say without reserva-
tion that he is well pleased with you." This is the level
of sanctification we are called to in Christ. Total and
complete transformation. This is what it means when
the Scriptures say, "Work out your salvation with fear
and trembling, for it is God who works in you, both to
will and to work for His good pleasure" (Philippians
2:12-13). Christ's ultimate will in your life is for you to
bring Him glory, and part of what it means to bring
God glory is embracing the sanctification process of
becoming more like Him. But I love the second part
of that verse. I do not know about you, but there are
many times when I become discouraged by the war
raging in me against my own flesh. It is a comfort to
know God's work in us is not only because it is His will
in us, but as Paul says, He takes pleasure in working
in us. He is totally committed to the process. Even if
that involves dealing with the biggest, most nefarious,
and chronic sin patterns in your life. It is His will, His
commitment, and His pleasure to work until they are
eradicated in our lives.

To walk with Christ is to walk in the already and not
yet. The "already" of being identified as holy before

God because of Christ's righteousness bestowed to us at the cross. And the "not yet" of learning to live our new identity out in the process of sanctification.

To walk in the already and not yet, is not a suggestion but a directive. We see this call of God on our lives in the book of 1 Peter: "For it is written, 'you shall be holy, for I am holy'" (1:16). Peter, in this section, is reminding his audience of the call to be holy by referencing the Old Testament. When Moses was giving the Law to the people of Israel, God often would give a series of commands of how the people would live and cap off the directive with, "You shall be holy for I am holy," (Leviticus 19:2; 20:7,26; 21:8; Exodus 19:6). God was not only giving His people behaviors to mimic, He was also calling out their heart. He did not desire them to act a certain way, but to be a certain way. He called them to be holy. Just as He was holy.

The same call stretches out to us. To be a Christian is to walk in the already and not yet. It is to kill our old nature, every piece of unholiness in us so we may be holy not only in name and in position before Christ but in every aspect of our being.

In order for us to fight against our deepest issues, we must first realize at the cross we are totally forgiven and redeemed. The power of sin in our life has been defeated, its shackles shattered, and our identity changed. It is with this knowledge we are able to walk forward in victory and truly change.

C H A P T E R   4

THE MIRROR

I watched this movie called *Ready Player One*. It is a film about a dystopian future where everyone spends their time in this virtual reality game called "The Oasis" to escape the atrocity of their real lives. The real world in this story is full of poverty and rugged wastelands, but in the game you can be anyone, go anywhere, do anything. It is a place of limitless potential, and it is a means of distraction from the real world. Inside this world, one can take their avatar to any planet or fandom that one could think of or interact with the countless 80's and 90's references sprinkled throughout the game. People in this story spend their entire savings and life earnings for rewards in the game because their true reality is so horrible and empty, they are willing to do anything to escape it.

While we do not live strapped into virtual reality goggles tangled in wires and apparatus, pining over a game, we do live in an age of distraction. In many ways, we find our lives boring or horrifying, and we seek to numb the experiences with our distractions. James, the brother of Jesus, writes in his epistle about being a doer of the Word instead of a hearer only. James compares it to one who looks in the mirror and then forgets what he looks like and carries on about his day. I think our distraction problem is much the same. We, in fact, are not all that much different from the people in *Ready Player One*. We distract ourselves so we do not have to look in the mirror. Because if we look in the mirror, we have to face our spiritual ugliness we are avoiding. If we look in the mirror, we have to face the emotions which threaten to pull us into the dark of depression. Forced to face the sin self-destructing our relationships and destroying the unity with our fellow man. One glance in the mirror, and we must respond to the injustice going on around us.

If we are going to live out practical righteousness, and grow into the image of Jesus, we must look in the mirror and deal with our core issues, no matter how uncomfortable and scary it may feel in the moment.

We live in a society of self-avoidance that craves distraction. We are in an overly media-saturated age. Countless TV shows, movies, video games, podcasts, audiobooks, music, and social media outlets lie at our fingertips, a second away from our grasp. We have a product to fill up every moment of our silence. In the car between work and home, there are countless podcasts to catch up on. Mowing the lawn becomes a venue to listen to an audiobook. While we wait for a friend at a coffee shop, we scroll aimlessly through our social media pages. When we do get done with all of our work for the day, we can pull out our phone and are catapulted into countless worlds. According to a study conducted by the tech giant Asurion, it is estimated Americans check their phones eighty to ninety-six times each day, which is once every ten minutes.

Our consumption has not been without effect on society. In 2015, a study done by Microsoft revealed our attention spans have decreased dramatically. Before the year 2000, studies conducted estimated our attention span was around twelve seconds. However, the more recent study by Microsoft estimated our attention spans are around eight seconds. For a frame of reference, the attention span of a goldfish is nine seconds. We are approaching and have already arrived at a place in our culture where we experience our lives through the lens of a screen rather than authentic living. I cannot help but get this feeling that our attention spans shrinking has less to do with an anticipation of getting new content and technology, as it is an avoidance of something else.

This is not another piece to hate on technology in society. The question I wish to pose here is how much of our consumption is based out of the fear of facing reality? We fill our free spaces with social media and content, not only because we are living in a media-saturated age, but because when we sit in the silence we are forced to interact and deal with the core issues in our lives.

In our culture, we have lost the art of being. Recently, I went on a vacation with my wife, Amanda. It had been a stressful season for my wife and I. Between finishing up her master's degree, and pastoring through some difficult circumstances at my church, we experienced a copious amount of stress. So we decided to take a few days to get away. During the first two days of our vacation, I would try to sit and relax, to enjoy a book or journal or enjoy a sunset from the hotel patio. But I could not get the crawling stress out of my chest. I felt *guilty* for not using the time to accomplish something or catch up on my favorite shows I had not had time to watch in a while. In that moment, the idea of doing nothing felt like a waste of time or a squandering of resources. The idea of being, of existing, of moving, enjoying one another's time and company felt like I would miss out on content all my friends and peers were taking in. The idea of facing silence felt terrifying. My wife felt it too. And it was not until we actually took time to separate ourselves from the rat race of everything and slow down that we realized how much we were caught up in it. To be honest, it took me two days to start relaxing and actually be comfortable with the silence of nothing going on.

It reminded me of being back in driver's training, and my bushy mustachioed driving instructor looking over and explaining velocitation to all of us in the car. After driving on the highway, it is easy to become accustomed to the speed of the freeway and the zipping of cars flying past. When leaving the freeway and adjusting to a slower speed, it can take a minute for your body to adjust to the new speed. It can feel like you are driving way slower than what you actually are going. In fact, if one is not careful, it can be easy to slip above the speed limit to match the old speeds on the highway. In the same way, we often have a tendency to take a while to slow down—to take time to just be.

Have we ever stopped to ask why we need to be plugged in? Why we are so uncomfortable with the silence in our head? Why do we feel the tightening of our chest cavities when there is no content to stream and nothing to distract us from the reality of our lives?

I believe we are terrified of being bored. And not only because we are afraid boredom is synonymous with failing to live a life well-lived. We are terrified of that moment when there is nothing to distract us from the heartache and the emptiness inside us. Because the moment we are bored and left alone to our thoughts, we have to face the void in our own chests. It is in the silence we are reminded of our lust and anger or the fear of losing control in the various aspects of our lives. Maybe we are terrified of failing. Somewhere along the line, we have believed the lie if we can just keep ourselves entertained long enough that maybe, just maybe, we can forget the issues plaguing us and the realities we do not wish to face each morning. Much like the old adage, "Out of sight, out of mind," we believe if we forget about our issues and distract ourselves from reality, maybe those things will not affect us so much.

The problem is that most of our issues do not depart from us like a forgotten acquaintance. In one of his novels, Neil Gaiman said, "Wherever you go, you take yourself with you."[5] We cannot outrun ourselves or hide from our issues; they follow wherever we go, even when we bury them under layers of entertainment and comfort.

Our cultural obsession with striving to be entertained often is a side effect of a deeper problem of avoiding the issues that are going on in our lives. If we are going to face our old nature and grow into the image of who God has called us to be, we have to face the silence and look in the mirror. We have to be present in the midst of the pain rather than just suppress and ignore it. The practical righteousness we talked about in the last chapter does not happen in a

vacuum. Sanctification happens when we intentional-
ly lean into the process of growth.

Another reason I believe we chase after entertainment and distraction is because we believe that is
what will make us happy. We do not have to face the
negative things in our lives, and we can do something
enjoyable and fun. Our society worships attempts at
happiness, however short or long those feelings last.
Our culture tells us to chase after what makes us happy, and nothing can stand in the way of what makes
us happy. However, in our search for happiness, we
have lost joy.

As a culture, most of us think joy and happiness are
synonymous. And while they can share some similari-
ties, there are stark differences. Happiness is a mood.
It is an emotion which comes and goes based upon
circumstance. Happiness is pulling up to the Chick-
fil-A drive-thru and the red uniformed worker handing
you a steaming hot paper bag with chicken and waffle
fries—all of it dripping in the delectable nectar known
as Chick-fil-A sauce. Happiness also ends when you
eat the last bite. It is dependent on our circumstances
and can change in a moment's notice. It is there one
moment and disappears the next.

Joy is different. It is not so much an emotion as
it is a posture. It is not something dependent on circumstances; joy is an embracing of a perspective
completely alien to our own. In James 1:2-3, the writer

says, "Consider it joy, when you meet trials of various kinds, because you know that the testing of your faith produces steadfastness." He says to consider it joy when the difficult times come and the moments of silence where you are too afraid to look in the mirror because you are afraid of what you may see. In the moments when the doctor comes in with bad news, when your parents split, when your friends betray you, or when you do not know if you are going to be able to make ends meet. When you look at the issue in your life that you believe cannot change, he says to consider it joy.

In fact, the people James is writing to in this particular passage are being persecuted for their faith. We do not know exactly to what extent the persecution is taking place, but we know it is bad enough that many Christians were forced to leave their homes and be scattered into the surrounding cities and nations. They were losing their property, losing their jobs, and it is possible some of them were even losing their lives and loved ones.

Consider it joy.

He does not say to consider it joy because the situations are fun or enjoyable. Rather, he says to consider them joy because of something else entirely. He says to consider it joy because, "You know that the testing of your faith produces steadfastness." The joy does not come from the circumstances, which may be grueling and life altering; the joy comes from the coming end result of what story God is telling in the midst of it. The trial and heartache is not something God brings into our lives in order to crush us. When these events come into our lives, they can transform us.

But unless we look in the mirror, we are not able to be transformed. In fact, James continues, "And let steadfastness have its full effect, that you may be perfect and complete lacking in nothing" (1:4). We have to lean into the process. We have to live a life unafraid of the silence. We have to face it. We have to look into the mirror of silence. Stare at the things we would rather ignore and consider it joy.

Before Jesus went to the cross or sweated blood in the Garden, He asked for any other way for the redemption of mankind. However, the road to the cross was the one path to the salvation of mankind, and He leaned into the process. He also found joy. The writer of Hebrews says, "Looking to Jesus, the founder and perfecter of our faith, who for the joy that was before him endured the cross, despising the shame, and is seated at the right hand of the throne of God" (12:2). The cross itself was not joy. Jesus did not enjoy the nails which were driven through his hands, the slap of the cat o' nine tails, or a crown of thorns violently twisted on His head. But He saw the end result. He saw the rivers of blood bathing and cleansing a hundred billion souls. He saw creation being righted and death working backwards. It was resting in God's definition of good that Jesus was able to carry the splintering cross, step by bloody step, to its conclusion. Joy is resting in God's definition of good.

He considered it joy.

We are called to adopt Jesus' mindset. Living in the ignorance of our problems or sin, because we do not wish to face them, does not make them disappear. We must look in the mirror and not just hear Christ's call on our life to pick up our cross and follow Him. We must bend down, let our hands feel the roughness and prickliness of the cross, and carry it too.

I used to be afraid of the mirror. I hated seeing the ugliness—and so often the same ugliness. The same issue of pride. The same insecurity. The same marring wound of lust. I would dive into my hobbies and busy myself—rather than confronting my pain, I had a tendency to numb and suppress it. It is easy in this mindset to start blaming God while we numb the pain and fill the silence with a raucous of sound. It was not until I started to see God in the midst of my pain that I began to see things in a much different light.

The solution to our problem, it seems, is the opposite of what feels comfortable. We must stop avoiding the sins and problems in our lives and admit that they exist. If we are constantly avoiding or distracting ourselves from the problems and never allow ourselves to truly evaluate ourselves, then we will not change. We must embrace the silence and look in the mirror. We can gaze upon our reflection, the bruises, scrapes, cuts, and diseases included, and feel the ache and sorrow and everything we hate in us. To consider it joy by focusing on God's definition of good and lean into the process of transformation. This is not a transformation done by our own will or ability but one born of the Spirit. Lean in and consider it joy.

CHAPTER 5

A BETTER SONG

In 1510 AD, Martin Luther would climb large staircases on his knees reciting prayers on each step as an effort to redeem his life from purgatory. This practice can still be observed on the stairs of the Scala Sancta in Rome. In India, devotees to the Hindu religion gather for the Thaipusam festival for an offering to Lord Murugan. During this festival, they will petition for forgiveness, health, and other requests during the new year. During this festival, they will pierce themselves with hooks and skewers throughout their whole body to show their devotion to Murugan. They believe their god will listen to them based on their sincerity and willingness to hurt and maim themselves. We like the idea of severity to the body. Thousands of years of manmade religion tells us that. It makes us feel like we are in control and earning something. It is a human measurement of growth that shows we in ourselves are strong and have what it takes. Most of us in Christendom do not throw hooks in ourselves or climb stairs on our knees to show our devotion. However, we do often practice physical effort to earn God's love.

Growing up in the conservative church culture, I read a lot of books about dealing with temptation focused on the physical things people have to do in order to overcome those sins which easily beset us. A lot of the strategies revolved around avoiding places "where sin lived." Avoid going to the movies because some of the movies were bad. Avoid secular music because the beat was set to the tune of satanic cadence. Avoid going to the mall because some women wore low-cut shirts. Much like the contemporary church's view of salvation—a divine escapism focusing on a goal of escaping to paradise and leaving behind a damned world—much of the modern church's view of conquering sin revolves around the same escapist tendencies and focuses on our own strength and human-based effort.

It is not to say many of these strategies are born of ill intentions. They are often born out of a human conception of trying to do the right thing, albeit mustered from human effort. It is much like the Christians in Colossae caught up in legalistic tenancies that Paul addresses:

If with Christ you died to the elemental spirits of the world, why, as if you were still alive in the world, do you submit to regulations—'Do not handle, Do not taste, Do not touch' (referring to things that all perish as they are used)—according to human precepts and teachings? These have indeed an appearance of wisdom in promoting self-made religion and asceticism and severity to the body, but they are of no value in stopping the indulgence of the flesh. (Colossians 2:20-23)

In Jesus' time, there were religious leaders by the name of the Pharisees. They were comparable to a pastor today. They were large proponents for the synagogue movement, insisting the temple was not just used for ritual worship but was also a place for instruction and learning about Jehovah on a daily occurrence. While they enforced rules clearly defined in the Torah (the first five books of the Old Testament), they also believed the source of truth was not only in the written word but also in the oral tradition God passed down to the people. This led to the writing of the Mishnah—a collection of sermons which clarified and interpreted the Torah. In these pages, they would add restrictions to the law to help keep the Israelites from straying from God. An example of this would be the view of the Sabbath. Due to the fourth commandment, the Jews were not supposed to work on Saturdays. The Mishnah added thirty-nine categories for what "work" meant. And those categories were further divided into more categories. And these categories were divided into rules of how many steps could be taken on the Sabbath without being regarded as work, or how many letters one could write down on a page without slipping into working on the Sabbath. They added rules to the law of God, to show the Israelites if they stayed in the lines drawn by men, they would not fall into transgression.

The Mishnah was supposed to be a practical guide to what was approved by God and what was not approved by God. It was made with the best intentions—to lead the people into the holiness into which God called them. But rather than beckoning the people closer to God, it held the people of Israel back from Him. It bonded them to their sin even more. Because while guidelines are good, they are unable to quell the idea of sin in our heart. Rules can make some good guardrails, but they do not kill the sin in us. The Pharisees are not that different from how we often deal with our sin. We can avoid "where sin lives" all we want, but we cannot avoid the sin that lives within us.

When I was in college in Pennsylvania, the school I attended had a similar idea about dealing with sin. One could not hold the hand of their significant other on campus, because it could lead to a sexual encounter. Students had to be in their dorm by 10:30 at night, because to be out later meant that sinful activities could happen. R-rated movies could not be watched—even when going on break home with your family several states away. Rooms had to be cleaned daily and inspected by an RA (Resident Assistant). And do not even mention drinking. The motive behind the rules were made with the best intentions. The staff truly wanted students to know God and foster an environment where growth could happen. However, what ended up happening was a legalistic approach at sin. It became a mentality of: "What can I do that does not go over the line?" This even happened among the staff. Because rules, while necessary and helpful, do not create the self-control needed to stop the flesh. The gospel was never intended to only create those who follow rules while the heart longs for the things of the flesh. The gospel was meant to change us from the inside out.

There is an old myth about Odysseus in Homer's *Odyssey*. Odysseus was the king of Ithaca, and the poem recounts his journey home from the Trojan War. He was a cunning and arrogant man. At one point in the journey, he stopped along the way on an Island ruled by a nymph named Circe. She was lustrous and she turned all of Odysseus' crew into pigs with a potion. She only turned them back to normal when the hero agreed to have a tryst with her. After she turned his men back to their normal selves, she warned him of the journey ahead. She mentioned the next encounter on their journey would be the Sirens. The Sirens sang a song which lured the hearts of men toward it. It sounded beautiful and sultry, and those who heard it would become transfixed and go to all lengths to get to it. But the end of it was death. As soon as the sailors came close enough to the sound, they would be killed by the Sirens. After warning him about the danger Circe told him,

> *Drive your ship past the spot, and to prevent any of your crew from hearing, soften some beeswax and plug their ears with it. But if you wish to listen yourself, make them bind you hand and foot on board and stand you up by the step of the mast, with the rope's ends lashed to the mast itself. This will allow you to listen with enjoyment to the twin Sirens' voices. But if you start begging your men to release you, they must add to the bonds that already hold you fast.[6]*

Circe, knowing Odysseus was a man driven by his passions, threw a line of temptation out to the hero to be able to safely protect his crew, while he would be able to hear the song without dying to its sultry call. He had the option to put beeswax in his own ears to pass safely past the area, but he craved the song itself. He craved the desire to be able to say he survived the Siren song. And so he went. His men journeyed on the sea until they reached the Isle of the Sirens. He followed the orders of Circe: he put beeswax in the ears of his men and instructed them to tie him to the mast of the ship and not to untie him no matter how much he cried out to them. They obeyed. And the Sirens began to sing:

Odysseus, bravest of heroes,
Draw near to us, on our green island,
Odysseus, we'll teach you wisdom,
We'll give you love, sweeter than honey.
The songs we sing, soothe away sorrow,
And in our arms, you will be happy.
Odysseus, bravest of heroes,
The songs we sing, will bring you peace.[7]

The songs the Sirens sang pulled at the innermost desires of Odysseus, calling to his vanity, desire, and drive for safety and a home. The text goes on to say that he wailed and wailed for his men to let him go to the source of the song, but his men tied him tighter to the mast, despite his screams. His response to the Sirens' song revealed the cravings of his heart.

So often, we come into the battles with our flesh much the same way. We subject ourselves to the temptations of our heart, load up on accountability, and grit our teeth and call it self-control. True self-control is not a tied-to-the-mast struggle where we force ourselves through the gritted teeth of human effort to avoid our sin. That is a pride-filled venture which does not impress or please a holy God. Accountability is good. Guard rails are good. But until we deal with the heart which desires to fall to the songs of Sirens, we are only living a life tied to a mast while we yearn for the things of this world. It looks like godliness, and it seems all very religious, but at the root of it, it is no different than the Pharisees creating rules to stop people from doing what they long to do.

The gospel not only gives us a new destination and a relationship with God, it reaches in and begins to change our desires away from longing for the flesh. It causes us to desire after the things of the Father. In fact, Scripture would go so far as to say we are dead to our sin. "Now those who belong to Christ Jesus have crucified the flesh with its passions and desires" (Galatians 5:24). When we lay our sin at the feet of Christ at our salvation, we are not only asking for the forgiveness of our transgressions, but we are laying down our entire heart. We are laying down our selfishness and pride and crucifying it on the cross with Jesus.

We cannot do this on our own, however. When we place our faith in Christ at salvation, we are given the Holy Spirit. One of the Spirit's roles in our lives is to conform us to the image of Christ. One of the ways the Holy Spirit does this is by helping us kill our sin. In the book of Romans, Paul says, "For if you live according to the flesh you will die, but if by the Spirit you put to death the deeds of the body, you will live. For all who are led by the Spirit of God are sons of God" (8:12-14). The Holy Spirit's role in our struggle with sin is vital to the process. In another part of Scripture, Paul says, "For God gave us a spirit not of fear, but of power and love and self-control" (2 Timothy 1:7). It is through the Holy Spirit's power and influence in our life we can experience freedom from the influence and power of sin.

This does not mean it is easy. This does not mean all you have to do is pray a prayer and your sin will magically no longer be a struggle. Crucifying our flesh is a daily posture of handing over our will and desires, so the will of the Father may happen in and through us. We cannot remove ourselves from the world of temptation. There are numerous Scriptures which talk about the fact that temptation will come. Our sinful hearts will rear their ugly heads. We all have vices the Spirit works to sanctify. Temptation is going to come. But not only is God after our actions and ceasing from sin, He is seeking to change what we love and what our hearts yearn for.

There is this verse in the book of James that says this: "Submit yourselves therefore to God. Resist the devil, and he will flee from you" (4:7). I used to focus hard in on the phrase, "Resist the devil, and he will flee." I would grit my teeth, yell at Satan, quote Bible verses, and try to get my mind off of my temptations.

But there is another key phrase in that verse, a prerequisite to effectively dealing with our sin: "Submit yourselves therefore to God." When the temptation comes, we do not grab the steering wheel and take off on our own misadventure of resistance. We bow the knee to a God who can do more than all we ask (or think) and surrender. To let go of the notion we are the one fighting this battle, or we are strong enough. It is only when we first submit ourselves and relinquish control of our flesh, we can actually fight the battle with our sin.

Jesus famously says in chapter 15 of the book of John: "I am the vine; you are the branches. Whoever abides in me and I in him, he it is that bears much fruit, for apart from me you can do nothing" (15:5). Branches, by nature, only live by drawing on the nutrients of the vine. I think it is easy in our American, individualistic mentality, to be offended by Jesus telling us apart from Him we can do nothing. But this verse is a call to the inward parts of us; not only were we not designed to do this by ourselves, but there is a mighty strength God is providing in the midst of our lack.

What about when we sin? As the book of Romans says, "There is therefore now no condemnation for those who are in Christ Jesus. For the law of the Spirit of Life has set you free in Christ Jesus from the law of sin and death. For God has done what the law, weakened by the flesh, could not do" (8:1-3). When we fall to the song of the Sirens—and as I look at my life, how often I fall—we do not have a Father in heaven who stands to condemn us. We have an advocate who stands and says, "This child is mine." His blood speaks a better word, one of forgiveness. When we fall into sin, our positional righteousness before God, based on Christ's righteousness, remains steadfast. For the believer, our temptation with sin is no longer a struggle of condemnation or the possibility of falling from salvation. Temptation for the believer is entering into the process of conformity to Jesus. Temptation, by itself, is not condemnation of a life being lived wrongly; it is a test of our character and of what we are going to choose to love. Our temptation to sin is a further invitation to come and take part in a better song than the song of the Sirens.

Odysseus was not the only captain to sail past the isle of the Sirens. There is another man in Greek mythology who conquered this feat. Jason, in the tale of the Golden Fleece, led the Argonauts through the area. Rather than stuffing the beeswax into the ears of everyone on the ship, Jason had another plan. Orpheus, one of his men, hearing the sultry songs of the Sirens, pulled out his lyre and began to sing. The song he sang was more beautiful and more transfixing than the bewitching songs of the Sirens. The sailors were able to move past the islands of the Sirens because the song they listened to was more beautiful than the sound of temptation.

The gospel is the better song which provides a better way to overcome temptation. The love of Christ is the better melody beckoning us to submission in the midst of a world where a million melodies call for our attention. C.S. Lewis once said:

> *It would seem that Our Lord finds our desires not too strong, but too weak. We are half-hearted creatures, fooling about with drink and sex and ambition when infinite joy is offered us, like an ignorant child who wants to go on making mud pies in a slum because he cannot imagine what is meant by the offer of a holiday at the sea. We are far too easily pleased.*[8]

Our desires are far too easily amused. Through the gospel, God is beckoning us into a deeper joy. A joy which when temptation crosses us, we bend the knee, call out to Him who loves us and enter into His rest because we love Him more than the temptation in front of us.

THE HOLLOW MEN IN THE WASTELAND

In 1925, British poet T.S. Eliot published a poem titled "The Hollow Men." It is a harrowing look at the post-World War I psyche. He wrote the piece after the Treaty of Versailles ended the war and Europe still felt the ravaging of war all across the continent. The people of Europe felt hollow. They had this shell of peace on their skin as the gunshots stopped. But as they looked around and saw all the bodies, all the casualties of war, and the depth of man's depravity, everyone wondered if there really was much hope left in the world. Victory had come, but at what cost? Eliot, during this time, additionally dealt with a divorce because his wife had an affair with another man. His personal hollowness took on a new form as he not only dealt with the existential horror of the aftermath of the war, but he also had the horror of personal loneliness and betrayal.

In the poem, he speaks to the hollowness that he, and much of mankind, felt in the wake of all the loss. Eliot poignantly paints the picture of our vanity. I think there are a lot of times when we are young where we think we are invincible. We think whatever we set our minds to we can accomplish. When we realize our dreams of what we feel our life should be like will not come to fruition, it can cause us to feel directionless and hollow.

The reason I bring up "The Hollow Men" is I believe there are seasons of our spiritual lives where we feel hollow, like we are walking in the wastelands. When I first started to walk with God, it felt like I had exploded with new life. I had new desires. I wanted to be in God's Word all the time. I wanted to pray, often sneaking away from my family for hours to pray. I could not wait for Sunday, because Sunday was the day I got to sing to God with other people and listen to sermons and reflect on what God was saying. Those desires were totally new to me. In addition, I was seeing answers to prayer of real needs in my life. I felt like Adam in the Garden, walking and talking with God. It felt like I could almost reach out and touch God. I look back on those years and see my faith being constructed brick by brick.

However, when I turned eighteen, a poignant moment happened in my life where it felt like God took a step back. It felt like when I showed up to the Garden to walk with Him and He missed the appointment. Those intense desires to dive into Scripture and go to church started to subside. The Garden I had come to enjoy so much had turned into a wasteland.

I still read the Bible, went to church, and lived out my faith as best I could. But the desert seemed to just stretch on and on. It felt like the color had been snatched away. I was scared to open up to anyone in my life. I was afraid people may think I was not truly a Christian, or they might pry into my life because they thought there was some secret sin I was holding. Honestly, when this season started, the first thing I checked and sought God on was if there was some sin in my life or something of which I had not repented. While there are many places in Scripture where we are commanded to look at our heart and examine ourselves, I could not find a sin causing what I was experiencing.

Sometimes, in the midst of chasing after change in our lives, we will go through periods of spiritual drought. They can be frightening and disorienting, but they are vital in the process of unknotting our old nature. When people come to my office for counseling, almost all of them will inevitably say at some point, "Davis, I can't feel God right now. He feels distant." When people say something like this, there is usually a tight look across their face like they just said a curse word. My response to them is always the same: "Well, the first question we have to ask is, is there a reason, or is this a season?"

Sometimes the dry spells in our lives happen when we fall into a pattern of sin and it hardens us to God. It hardens us to other people. It may not seem like it is affecting us much at the beginning, but as time goes on we start to realize that there is no hunger for the Word of God anymore. In the Scriptures, David is a prime example of this. In 2 Samuel 11, we see David out on his rooftop surveying his kingdom. If he was honest, he should not have even been there. His armies were out in combat, and he was supposed to be with them. But he stayed. While he looked out across his kingdom, he saw a beautiful woman bathing on a rooftop below. He saw her, wanted her, and went out and got her. He thought he had gotten away with it until she came to him later and said she was pregnant. David then found out she was married to Uriah, one of David's captains at war. Most people at this point would be freaking out and terrified. But David had a plan. He sent for Uriah to get an update on what was happening in the campaign. After the update was finished, David told Uriah to go home and spend time with his wife. Uriah left the chambers, but did not go home. For he did not feel like it was fair for him to enjoy the company of his wife while his men were fighting and dying in another land.

David had to get sneaky. He gave Uriah a letter to give to Joab, the commander of the army. In the letter, David ordered Uriah be put on the front lines of the fighting, in the most dangerous place (2 Samuel 11:15). Joab obeyed, and Uriah was killed. Once David received the news, he married Bathsheba. The last verse of the chapter says, "The thing that David had done displeased the Lord" (2 Samuel 11:27). This caused a dry spell, which separated David from intimacy with God. It is impossible for us to maintain a healthy relationship with God when there is unrepentant sin in our lives. It was not until Nathan the prophet came and confronted David on what he had done that David even faced it. He repented and his intimacy was restored. In Psalm 51:10-12, he wrote about his repentance:

> *Create in me a clean heart, O God, and renew a right spirit within me. Cast me not away from your presence and take not your Holy Spirit from me. Restore to me the joy of your salvation, and uphold me with a willing spirit.*

The only way out of a dry spell caused by sin is through repentance. Repentance in Scripture means to simply "turn around." It means to cease one activity and pick up another. If we are holding onto bitterness or caught in adulterous lust, it is impossible to maintain intimacy with God until we turn from these things. When dry spells come up in our lives, it is important to seek and ask God if there is any sin in us to repent from. Psalm 139:23-24 talks about this: "Search me, O God, and know my heart! Try me and know my thoughts! And see if there be any grievous was in me, and lead me in the way everlasting!" The writer asked God to reveal the sin in his life so he may confess it and turn away from it. One of the Holy Spirit's roles is to reveal our sin so we can repent.

Another reason for our spiritual dry spells can be misplaced affections. Oftentimes we let other things take over the throne of our hearts. Sometimes we let things which are not bad things, like hobbies, family, or careers, take the chief seat of authority in our lives. We let good things take places in our lives they were never meant to play. When we fashion good things into idols, and we place idols on the thrones of our lives, we may struggle to hear God. This is not happening because He is no longer speaking but because we are tuned in to the voice of our idol instead. The solution to this type of dry spell is the same: repentance. It is admitting we have misplaced our priorities and put things above Christ, no matter how good or innocent the "thing" is. We must put our idols back in their rightful places, and Christ in His rightful place.

However, sometimes it is not sin or an idol causing the dry spell; sometimes it is a season. C.S. Lewis, upon the death of his wife, recounted one such dry spell in his book *A Grief Observed*:

> *When you are happy, so happy that you have no sense of needing Him, so happy that you are tempted to feel His claims upon you as an interruption, if you remember yourself and turn to Him with gratitude and praise, you will be—or so it feels—welcomed with open arms. But go to Him when your need is desperate, when all other help is vain, and what do you find? A door slammed in your face, and a sound of bolting and double bolting on the inside. After that, silence.[9]*

Lewis went on throughout this work to talk about the colossal grief that he went through after his wife passed. However, while this book provided comfort and a sense of camaraderie for those who are going through grief and trauma, this book is really about Lewis' journey of doubt in the midst of a spiritual desert.

I once heard a talk at a missionary kid conference about walking with God. The lecturer talked about how when we first walk with Christ, we often feel like we are walking close with Him. Like a honeymoon phase of a relationship, everything feels electric. Then the speaker said, some seasons it feels like Jesus stops and says to you, "Keep walking." That was the first time I heard our times in the wasteland are normal and not always tied to sin. The times in the wasteland were actually testing times. It was not an abandonment of God, so I could be picked over by the vultures; it was an invitation for a deeper intimacy with Him.

I think the temptation for us in the midst of our dry spells is to wish to go back to the way things were before the desert began. In fact, so many of our worship songs in America today are about asking God to take us back to the beginning where our love for Him was fresh, and we had all these warm feelings toward God. Where it felt like God was close. But have we ever stopped to ask the question that maybe God does not want us to go back to the way things were with Him? What if He desires our faith to keep moving forward? What if He wants our faithfulness in dryness? Sometimes, I think we wish we could go back because it would be easier. The truth, however, is we do not need to go backward; we need to go deeper.

Since I was eighteen, I have had many seasons in the wasteland. Some of them have been short, and some have dragged for months or longer. And if there is anything I have learned by walking through them, it's this: the only way out is through. The only way out is to lean in and embrace the wasteland as a provision from God to stretch us and change us to be like His Son.

I have a friend named Jason; we met in college. We hit it off during my sophomore year, and it did not take us long to be spiritual brothers. I remember one night, we were talking late into the night and were sharing our life stories and the current things we were going through. After I finished telling him my upbringing, I told him about the season of dryness I was going through and how God felt silent and distant.

"Do you have any Ebenezer stones?" he asked.

"Ebenezer stones?" I said.

"Yeah. You know, spiritual monuments that help you remember what God has done in your past. When you struggle with doubt or feeling God's presence, it gives you something to look back on."

I had never really thought about it that way. For someone who has a bookshelf of journals where I have scribbled down what has happened in my life, I forget what happens quite easily. I forget the things God has done in my life in the past. I forget the answered prayer and the spiritual growth God has given. I often get caught up in the moment and lose sight of what God has done.

I know I am not the only one. In fact, looking back at the Old Testament, we find the Israelites. After wandering for forty years in the desert, we see them cross the Jordan River to head into the promised land. Unfortunately, the hard part was coming. Wandering in the desert had been difficult; the time of slavery had been difficult. But walking into the promised land was going to be the biggest test of faith yet. It was time to conquer cities.

However, before they went into the land, God had one more miracle for them. As they passed through the Jordan River, into the promised land, the water parted before them to let them pass on dry ground. God commanded Joshua to have his men grab twelve stones—one for each tribe of Israel—as a reminder of what God had done for them:

> *And Joshua said to them, "Pass on before the ark of your God into the midst of the Jordan, and take up each of you a stone upon his shoulder, according to the number of the tribes of the people of Israel, that this may be a sign among you." (Joshua 4:5-6)*

The passage goes on to say, additionally, when their children came to them in the future and asked about the stones, they could explain the faithfulness of God and all He had done. He wanted them to remember what He had done when they encountered resistance fighting against the nations of the land. In the midst of walking around the walls of Jericho. In the midst of the hard times when there weren't any crops growing in the fields. When the days of doubt came, and the darkness seemed to encroach all around them. He wanted them to be able to look back on those stones and remember His faithfulness to them. And it was not only for them. But it was for their children who were not present when the Israelites crossed the river.

God knows we are fickle. It is so easy for us to forget the past. I think our memory fades even more quickly in the dry times, like the desert sun evaporates the moisture of our faith. The past faithfulness of God on our horizons sometimes looks like distant mirages. We get caught up in the heat of the sun and the burning sand, rolling dunes, and the dryness of our tongues. We forget God is supreme over all. We forget the God of the greenest pastures is the God of the driest desert.

Do you have Ebenezer stones? Do you have memories you can look back on to remind you of God's faithfulness in the past? I have read of people who have painted answers to prayer on small stones and leave them in a jar on their kitchen counter. Every few months they go through them to remind themselves of God's faithfulness in their life. If we are going to survive our dry seasons, it is important to remember God's faithfulness to us in the past.

However, we not only need to remember what God has done in the past; we must also seek Him in the present. There is this awesome quote from *The Last Battle* by C.S. Lewis, when Jewel the Unicorn enters Aslan's country. "I have come home at last! This is my real country! I belong here. This is the land I have been looking for all my life, though I never knew it till now… Come further up, come further in!" [10]This idea of "further up and further in" by nature beckons the walker to move forward through the greenest pastures and through the driest deserts. No matter the landscape, it cannot be traveled backwards. We must go further up and further in.

I remember spending many sessions in prayer asking God to deliver me from the desert. I felt like Paul asking God to remove the thorn from my side. I thought it was a pretty good prayer. I was asking for deeper intimacy with God, after all. I was asking for grandiose feelings and zeal. But I did not get the answer I expected. It was not an audible voice, but it was there, still and small. "You don't own this desert." It was then I realized God not only owned the green country, but He owned all the deserts too. The God who walked with me and taught me in the good seasons of my life was the same God who walked with me in the desert. Just because I did not feel Him present with me, did not mean He was not present.

In the midst of my dry spells, I have had people tell me God might show up if I just had more faith. I used to feel really guilty I did not have enough faith. But does it not take more faith to be faithful in spite of not feeling Him? Does it not take more faith to walk day by day even when we do not feel God? We live in a culture that loves our feelings. I think we could say we often worship our feelings. We love to be moved by emotion and experience. In fact, so many of the popular worship bands of today seem to emphasize the experience of worship above the experience of God. While there is nothing wrong with feelings, they make bad masters.

How often are we more attracted to the feeling of God than God Himself? Jesus has promised He will never leave nor forsake us (Matthew 28:20), and if we draw close to Him, He will draw near to us (James 4:8). These two promises are true whether we feel them or not. The Scriptures, however, actively tell us not to lean on our feelings. Scripture says our, "Hearts are deceitful above all else" (Jeremiah 17:9), and, in another place, to, "Trust in the Lord with all your heart and lean not on your own understanding" (Proverbs 3:5).

In fact, it is most often in the midst of these times in the desert I am reminded of God's promises. In Psalm 119 the writer says, "This is my comfort in my afflic-tion, that Your promise gives me life" (Psalm 119:50). The writer here is saying in the midst of the hard times in his life, where feeling is not present, he is forced to lean on God's promises. Charles Spurgeon once said somewhere, "I have learned to kiss the waves that throw me against the Rock of Ages." I used to hate the desert. But I have learned the dry times in our faith are just another set of waves throwing me into the Rock.

In the midst of the wasteland, keep seeking. On the days where you feel like seeking God feels worthless, seek anyway. During the times when it feels like your prayers bounce off the ceiling, pray anyway. When it feels like going to church is an empty exercise, go anyway. God calls us onward in the midst of the wasteland. As we mentioned earlier, the only way out is through. And just like a couple chapters ago when we talked about how spiritual growth takes intentional movements, walking through the desert seasons takes intentional movement as well.

When I am in the desert, I find the Psalms to be my constant companions. Many of the Psalms are written by people who are crying out because they feel as though God were distant. They were written in the midst of drought, pain, and doubt. What I love about the Psalmists is even in the midst of their worst seasons of life they continue to seek God in the midst of the struggle. Read and pray Psalm 57, 63, 13, or many others written by worn-out people seeking God in the midst of their troubling seasons.

Finally, in the midst of the wasteland, keep waiting. This is the hardest part of walking through dry seasons. Even after going through many deserts, I never enjoy it. But I have learned to submit to the process in the moment. There has never been a dry spell in my life where God has not been faithful and led me back into green pastures. Remember the words of Paul: "We do not lose heart, though our outer self is wasting away, our inner self is being renewed day by day" (2 Corinthians 4:16). This is not only true on the days when we feel like we are changing and growing;

it is also true in the midst of the driest desert. He is constantly shaping and remaking you.

In your desert seasons, focus on God's promises. Meditate on the times God has been faithful in the past, and use them as fuel to believe God will be faithful in the present. Keep seeking and pursuing Him, even when on the days it feels like a lost cause. In the midst of it all, keep waiting.

T.S. Eliot wrote another poem titled "The Wasteland." It is a dense poem best read with commentaries present. Throughout the piece he contrasts life and death and how society has not turned out the way he thought. Mankind was capable of much more darkness than he thought imaginable. According to him, the journey of life is much more like a wasteland than a garden. There are many sections of life that feel like a wasteland. But we are not the hollow men in the wasteland—we are not the stuffed men full of straw. God is just as present in our feelings of distance in the wasteland, as He is in the midst of the greenest garden. And whether we walk through the desert or the verdant pastures, God will bring His children home.

BRAIDED CORDS

As I write this chapter, I am in the corner of a coffee shop waiting for someone who requested to meet with me. A couple days prior, I had received a text from a young man in our church. He had been grieved by the loss of his sister and grandfather several years prior. Once he arrived, we had small talk for a couple minutes before I asked him what he wanted to talk about. He told me of his sister's passing, then subsequently his grandfather's. Then, with tears in his eyes, "I just want to know why it happened. I don't like to admit this, but I'm angry at God for taking them." There was a tight silence then in the air for a second. He looked as though admitting his anger toward God out loud would cause me to reject him, maybe God too.

We still have one essential thing yet to discuss when it comes to the different aspects of change. We have spent time talking about several aspects of how we change, largely focusing on our vertical relationship to God, and how the gospel is the essential element in dealing with our deepest issues. All of these aspects could be summed up together to say that in order to change we must be vulnerable with God. We must admit we are unable to change on our own and are dependent on Him to help us change. But there is still one more important element in fighting against our old nature we need to talk about: vulnerability with other believers. If we are going to change, we need one another.

In the book of Ecclesiastes, the teacher wrote about our need for one another:

> *Two are better than one, because they have a good reward for their toil. For if they fall, one will lift up his fellow. But woe to him who is alone when he falls and has not another to lift him up! Again, if two lie together, they keep warm, but how can one keep warm alone? And though a man might prevail against one who is alone, two will withstand him—a threefold cord is not quickly broken. (Ecclesiastes 4:9-12)*

The writer noted the reward for the toil of vulnerability: To fall and be unable to get up becomes manageable when you have someone there to lift you up and help you hobble to safety. Shivering in your bed at night in the middle of January when your heater blows out becomes a little warmer when you are curled up next to someone. And withstanding a two-hundred-and-fifty pound intruder is much easier when there are two of you than when you are alone. The ecosystem of vulnerability allows for a mutual helping of one another when troubling times arise. In fact, the writer bluntly talked about the positives of vulnerability: "A three-fold cord is not quickly broken." A braided rope can withstand much more pressure than a single strand of rope. The teacher in Ecclesiastes considered vulnerability the most logical and efficient choice.

For many of us, however, vulnerability can be intimidating. In our American culture, we love to talk about our individuality. We take pride in our self-sufficiency and our ability to provide for ourselves. We also are far too attached to the image we create of ourselves through our social media outlets. Our Instagram posts are filled with calculated pictures and reels of "our lives." Or at least the manipulated shards of our lives we allow others to see. To be vulnerable with others in many ways is to risk marring the image of ourselves we project to others.

We may intellectually agree with the writer of Ecclesiastes that braided cords are the strongest, that community with our fellow man makes us all stronger. But if we are often honest, we would much rather not open ourselves up that far. Because, if we are not careful, vulnerability can hurt.

To be honest with other people about the things waging war against us risks the fear of judgment from others. We often fear our tears, desperation, and struggling will be interpreted as weakness, ruining our reputation. In our American culture, we love to talk about pulling ourselves up by our bootstraps, about making something of ourselves on our own. Even in the Church, we have popularized phrases such as, "God helps those who help themselves." In many ways, American Christianity has neutered the need for one another by worshiping at the altar of self-sufficiency.

The problem with self-sufficiency is it runs counter to Scripture and God's intent for the church. Life is not just "Me and Jesus." There are far too many Scripture verses talking about our need for one another. In Scripture, we are told to: love one another (John 13:34); pray for and confess your sins to one another (James 5:16); bear one another's burdens (Galatians 6:2); not lie to one another (Colossians 3:9); stop passing judgment on one another (Romans 14:13); and many more. In fact, if you were to look through the Scriptures you would find fifty-nine "one another" commands talking about what our relationship to one another looks like. Community and vulnerability is not a suggestion for believers in Jesus; it is a command for us to walk in together.

The call for believers is much higher than self-sufficiency. In fact, Peter, in his first epistle, puts it this way:

> *You are a chosen race, a royal priesthood, a holy nation, a people for his own possession, that you may proclaim the excellencies of him who called you out of darkness into his marvelous light. Once you were not a people, but now you are God's people; once you had not received mercy, but now you have received mercy. (1 Peter 2:9-10)*

This passage is pregnant with significance. "Chosen race, royal priesthood, a holy nation, a people for his own possession," are all terms which show up in the Old Testament in Exodus 19 and Deuteronomy 7, when Moses is communicating with the people of Israel concerning God's relationship with them. God was sharing through Moses that He called Israel as a collective people group to be different, holy, and called out for His purpose. Peter was communicating that just as the people of Israel were called out as a people, so believers in Jesus are called out as a people to be different.

When you stepped into a personal relationship with Christ, you were not transported just into a right standing before God. You were transferred from a kingdom of darkness into a kingdom of light filled with other people who have been set free as well. A lot of times, as Americans, we look at some of the above terminology, "chosen race," "royal priesthood," "holy nation," and we think of these titles as adjectives describing ourselves only. But Peter here is not using the word "you" in the singular sense. He is using it in the plural. In fact, a more accurate English word here would be the Southern "ya'll."

A better phrasing would be, "Ya'll are a chosen race, a royal priesthood, a holy nation, a people for his own possession." To step into a relationship with Christ, by nature, is to step into a corporate body called the Church. First in the global sense of the word, identifying with God's people as a group, but secondly, on a more practical, relational level, in a physical group of people who are near you. People who are following Christ alongside you and can lift you up in prayer when you experience suffering, bear your burdens when you are weak, and confront you when you veer off course, as you do the same thing for them. All of it is bound up in love for one another.

In our church's small groups ministry, we studied Dietrich Bonhoeffer's *Life Together*. In the book, he talked about our desperate need for one another.

> *God has willed that we should seek and find His living Word in the witness of a brother, in the mouth of man. Therefore, the Christian needs another Christian who speaks God's Word to Him. He needs him again and again when he becomes uncertain and discouraged, for by himself he cannot help him-*

self without belying the truth. He needs his brother man as a bearer and proclaimer of the divine word of salvation. He needs his brother solely because of Jesus Christ. The Christ in his own heart is weaker than the Christ in the word of his brother; his own heart is uncertain, his brother's is sure.[11]

The Christ in his own heart is weaker than the Christ in the word of his brother; his own heart is uncertain, his brother's is sure. When our hearts do not know what to say, our brothers and sisters can speak into us. When we look at the train wreck, and we cannot see any hope amid the wreckage, that is the precise moment we need our brothers and sisters to speak into our lives. It is the precise moment God has given our brothers and sisters to us in the first place.

I remember a time in my undergraduate studies when I wrestled deeply with the validity of Christianity. Growing up in the Church, I had not given much thought to the idea that what I believed could be wrong. When I hit my freshman year in college and started to experience different worldviews, even at a Christian university, I began to question everything. I checked out a few books on apologetics from our library, reading them ravenously. I still felt unresolved, and it terrified me. Some mornings it felt difficult to even get out of bed. It felt like my faith I had put so much stock in was unraveling faster than I could grip it and put it back together.

I felt afraid to open up about my doubts to my new friends at school; I was terrified they would judge me or write me off. I finally told my roommate, Daniel, one day. I remember feeling the air leave my lungs as I unloaded everything. Daniel listened with a smile and a nod and said he had doubts too. And, in a moment, we became voices into one another. It was not long before I shared my doubts at a prayer night in my dorm room with several more friends. They did not judge me either. In fact, they prayed with me. They took the time to encourage me and jumped in the trenches with me. In many ways, in the times I did not have faith to stand on, they let me borrow theirs. When the Christ in my heart was weak, the Christ in the word of my brother was strong, sure, and steadfast.

I believe it was their influence and encouragement in those days that gave me the strength to keep going. I knew several other students at school who ended up going through similar existential struggles who ended up leaving the faith after graduation. For many of them, their struggles caused them to isolate from other believers. And isolation bred cynicism. I understand how many of my colleagues ended up at the conclusions they did, for I flirted with many of the same thoughts. It was in this season I learned during the difficult seasons of life was when I needed to be closer to the Church, not further.

But vulnerability is not just important in the trials that beat against us. But also when it comes to dealing with the temptations and sin issues that wage war against us. James puts it this way:

> *Is anyone among you suffering? Let him pray. Is anyone cheerful? Let him sing praise. Is anyone among you sick? Let him call for the elders of the church, and let them pray over him, anointing him with oil in the name of the Lord. And the prayer of faith will save the one who is sick, and the Lord will raise him up. If he has committed sins, he will be forgiven. Therefore, confess your sins to one another and pray for one another, that you may be healed. (James 5:13-16)*

There is healing which vulnerability brings. There is healing when you can look in the eyes of your brother and confess what has been happening in your life, knowing their response will be, "The gospel reaches even here." Knowing they will sit with you in the midst of the muck and mire and help you as you walk through it. I can think of so many occasions in my life where I have sat across from a friend and confessed an attitude or something I had said or done, and they pointed me back to the gospel. They would remind me Jesus' blood was still enough. It still cleansed, and it still reached even to someone like me.

God gave us one another so when the difficult seasons come, we would not be alone and the darkest nights would not be as dark. Not too long ago, we had some big storms roll through our area in Southwest Michigan. The storms came in late and knocked out our power for almost a full twenty-four hours. It was my week to preach, so I woke up in the morning to start prepping the Sunday message, but everything in the house was dark. The storm was still raging outside, and rather than the rays of the sun shining through our windows, the atmosphere was grey and brooding and the wind howled. I used the flashlight on my phone to rummage around the house for some candles, placing them in a semi-circle around my Bible and journal on the coffee table. The red glow of the candles created a ring of light so I could see to study. It was only when all the candles were assembled together that I could see clearly.

That is the role we have in one another's lives. It is by the light of one another we are able to clearly see. As Holy Spirit indwelled individuals, we come together to comfort one another when one member is down. We challenge each other when sin rears its head in our lives. We stand together in the midst of fiery temptations and trials. We take the transforming nature of the gospel to a hurting world. We bear burdens even when the going gets tough. That is what it means to be the Church with one another.

I know vulnerability in church may not be the easiest thing for many of us. The Church has not done everything right. In fact, some of you who may be reading this may cringe when I say the word "church." Maybe you were actively involved in a church that hurt you. Perhaps you had a leadership team more concerned about power than actually loving Christ. Or maybe a pastor who cared way more about his personal ego and how he looked on the stage rather than caring for people who were broken and hurting. Plenty of churches have claimed to create safe spaces for people to be vulnerable, only to mar, judge, stab, and cast away people who did so. These types of experiences in churches can cause us to want to write off the Church forever.

Trust that has been decimated can take a long time to rebuild. Being hurt while being vulnerable is a horrible experience. And when we are hurt because of our vulnerability, our natural inclination is to not put ourselves in a scenario like it ever again. However, the scary part, the important part, is even those of us who have been hurt by the Church cannot use that as an excuse to buttress ourselves from vulnerability.

It does not mean you will not need time to heal. It does not mean that you necessarily have to stay with that specific church—although attempting reconciliation is definitely a good step. We are called to step into community again—even after experiencing hurt.

We need to persevere even when our first attempts at vulnerability again feels like tiptoeing with trying to find someone trustworthy. We are called to enter back into community to grow together into stronger braided cords once again.

PART TWO

KILLING QUEENS

KILL THE QUEEN

I worked at a hardware store several years ago. My boss, Greg, would often take me around the store to teach me how to use the products I was selling. On one of these occasions, he taught me how to deal with ants. It was spring, and many customers had come in and told us they were having issues with ants on their countertops.

Greg took me to the insecticide aisle and picked up a can of spray with a giant, black ant on the label. "Most people, when they start to have ants in their house, grab something like this," he said, holding up the can. "They freak out because they see ants crawling all over their counters or kitchen floors, and they want a quick fix to get rid of the problem. So they spray this stuff everywhere, and it kills the ants in the house."

"Well, that's good, right?" I asked.

"Well, yes," he said. "But the issue is the next morning they find more ants crawling over their counters and floors. A lot of people just keep spraying the aerosol and killing the ants they see, never to really deal with the problem. You see, people can kill all the ants they want in their house, but there is a queen ant in the nest outside pumping out new ants all the time," he said, making a circular motion with his index finger. "If you want to get rid of the ant problem in the house, you have to kill the queen ant in the nest."

"How do you kill the queen? Do you need to track down the nest?" I asked.

"Nope. You just need one of these," he said. He set down the can of spray and held up a plastic case full of smaller cases of clear liquid. "This is a liquid trap. The sweet smell attracts the ants that are in the house. They take a sip, and it tastes good. So they call all their ant friends over to take a drink too. They all love it, so they take it back to the nest to give to their queen. The queen drinks the poison and dies. Once the queen ant is dead, the other ants die off within a week."

"So in order to kill the ants, you need to kill the queen?" I mumbled.

Sometimes in life there are those moments where it feels like you are out of your body eavesdropping on yourself. Where you know one conversation is taking place, but another conversation is happening just below the surface. It was at that moment I realized most of us handle our battle against sin the wrong way. We often wage war against our sin like the people who grabbed the aerosol spray and sprayed the ants crawling all over the counter, only to be dismayed to see them again the next day.

Often in our battle against the sin in our own lives, we stick to the surface issues. It is honestly easier to deal with the ants on the counter and not go for the queen in the nest. In our American society, we want the instant results, the tangible, instantaneous satisfaction. So we buy the pornography blockers, count to ten before we blow up at our kids, pray harder when someone cuts us off in traffic, memorize a couple Scripture verses for when we feel tempted, and vow to not talk about politics at the Thanksgiving dinner table. We would much rather put a choke collar on the physical manifestations of our sin issues, rather than actually finding out why we desire to lust after men or women on a screen. Or why we feel angry when someone cuts us off in traffic. Or why we feel robbed when our kids invade our five minutes of quiet time in the morning.

The truth is our sin goes so much deeper than only the physical manifestations of it. The physical act of lust, or yelling at our kids, or jealousy over our neighbor's new car is just the symptom of a much larger problem in our sinful heart. You could spend your entire life dealing with the physical manifestations of your sin and never experience victory, because you never took out the taproot.

If we want to deal with the sin in our lives, we do not need more rules or more resolve or to try harder. We need to remove the queen. The writer of Proverbs puts it this way: "The purpose in a man's heart is like deep water, but a man of understanding will draw it out" (Proverbs 20:5). Our hearts go far deeper than we would expect, and the intentions of our heart are not always clearly seen. That is why so often we go through life just dealing with the symptoms of our sin, rather than actually dealing with the real thing. It takes time to find the queens deep within our hearts. Many times, we would much rather spray the ants on the counter than kill the queens that nest deep within us.

But how do we kill a queen? How do we take down the issues which feel so close to us, like they are a part of us? If these issues were not present in our lives, then maybe we would feel a little less like ourselves. I once counseled a man who was wrestling through a core issue—a queen issue. He told me he did not know what life would be like without it. It felt so tied to himself that to be without it would be to lose a part of his identity. And maybe you have felt that way yourself. Maybe you have experienced anxiety or anger or depression in your life so severely, you cannot picture life without it. Maybe if it was removed, you would feel a little less like yourself.

And that is the point. When sin knots itself in a chokehold around our heart, it is going to feel like a part of us. In his book *The Great Divorce*, C.S. Lewis recounts a story of a man who has a lizard on his shoulder. It has been there so long, coiled and nestled on his shoulder, it has become a part of him. It is representative of the core issues that stick close to us. One could say it is a queen. In the story, an angel comes to have an exchange with this man. He says for the man to enter into paradise, he must let the angel kill the lizard on his shoulder. At first, the man is excited at the prospect; this lizard has been a nuisance for so long, and he truly does hate the thing. But then the lizard digs his claws into the man's shoulder and tightens his tail around the man's neck. The man backs away from the angel, insisting it is not as bad as what the angel is making it out to be. The angel remains calm and repeats it must die, but it can only die if the man is willing.

The problem with killing queens is they desperately do not want to die. And in our flesh, we will do everything it takes to keep them alive. Our queen issues often appear in the form of our idols. Tim Keller once defined an idol as:

> *Anything more important to you than God, anything that absorbs your heart and imagination more*

> *than God, anything that you seek to give you what only God can give. A counterfeit God is anything so central and essential to your life that, should you lose it, your life would feel hardly worth living."[12]*

Idols oftentimes take good things and mutate them into consuming, cruel things, all the while masquerading as our saviors. They cause us to be phantoms of the people God has called us to be.

Our queens transform our good desires into twisted needs. They change us from enjoying the love and affection of the people in our lives to a consuming need to be approved by them. They change a healthy relationship with our finances and careers to a dogged drive to be self-sufficient and basking in the prestige it brings. Our queens change us from humbly accepting life as it comes, to craving control and manipulating the people around us to conduct our will.

Turning away from our queens is more costly than a quick resolve to turn over a new leaf; this change requires a renovation of character. I wish I could say killing queens was easy. But at its core, it is like experiencing death. Paul talks about this in Colossians 3:5: "Put to death therefore what is earthly in you: sexual immorality, impurity, passion, evil desire, and covetousness, which is idolatry." God is not after us controlling our idols or making them stay quiet. He is after their utter annihilation in us.

That is what we are going to focus on in the second half of this book. We are going to look at some of the most common queens which have a tendency to reign in us, and talk about how to identify them in our lives and kill them. Because despite how entrenched and difficult our queens are in our lives, no matter how tyrannical their rule in our hearts, they are killable. In fact, God's will in your life is that they are killed (1 Thessalonians 4:3).

At the end of the story in *The Great Divorce*, the man allows the angel to kill the lizard on his shoulder. It is searingly painful, but something the man did not expect begins to happen. Not only does the lizard die and fall from his shoulder, it turns into a white stallion. The thing that was a vice and hindrance in his life becomes a vehicle on which he can ride into the new kingdom.

This is the level of redemption God desires to work in us. He is not only after the elimination of our sin, but He is in the process of redeeming our sins, every single one of them. God is not only creating stories of grace to show the glory of the gospel, but changing our desires to be the opposite of who we once were. Paul puts it this way: "Let the thief no longer steal, but rather let him labor, doing honest work with his hands, so that he may have something to share with anyone in need" (Ephesians 4:28). He says let the thief no longer use his hands to take something of value from another individual against their will. Rather, let his hands do honest work, so he may use those same hands to willingly give to others. God does not just call for a ceasing of an action, but a reformation of character that leads to new actions.

The first step in dealing with a queen issue is repentance, not making excuses for it, or trying to minimize it. We need to humbly and honestly come before the Father and turn away from it. Repentance is more than only saying sorry for something we have done. In order to repent, we have to hate the entire story we have been trying to live through our sin. It is more than apologizing for blowing up at your wife or watching a pornographic film. We have to hate the entire story we were telling by doing these things. We must reject the entire thing. That is repentance.

In order to repent, we must first believe that God can answer and fulfill our deepest longings. Nobody wrestles with sin or turns to an idol without a reason. We often believe that our idols will fulfill our voids and make us feel at rest. In order to repent, we must believe that God can fulfill the longings in our heart more than our attempts to do so.

The second step takes things to the next level. It is not just "putting off" our sin. We must, "Put on then, as God's chosen ones, holy and beloved, compassionate hearts, kindness, humility, meekness, and patience... and let the peace of Christ rule in your hearts" (Colossians 3:12,15). To cease from one action is to start another. To release an identity is to pick up another. To stop telling a story, is to start telling a new one.

It does not mean you will get it right all the time. Or that your queen will go away immediately. Some issues take years of humble submission and growth to deal with. But day by day, we submit these queens to Christ as we follow after Him.

I remember going home after that conversation with my boss at the hardware store. I pulled out my journal and wrote the conversation down so I could process what happened that day. That night I started a new chapter in my journal titled, "On Killing a Queen."

CHAPTER 9

A BURNING
MATTRESS

Untangling the Knot of Living for the Approval of Others

I like to be liked by people. Growing up, I was a pretty awkward kid. I was never in with the popular people. I had plenty of friends, but deep down I was always afraid they were going to leave me if they really got to know me.

One summer when I was about ten years old, I had this friend who lived next door named Jordan. He was about four years older than me, but we would still hang out. Jordan was cool. He was an athlete, funny, and the girls loved him. I really wanted Jordan to like me. In many ways, I felt like I *needed* him to like me. It felt as though to gain his approval meant I could gain anyone's. One day, while I was playing outside, I saw him dragging a mattress over to his family's fire pit. He waved and motioned for me to come over. I jumped the wire fence separating our yards and asked him what he was up to.

"My mom told me to burn this old mattress," he said, crouching over the small pit lighting a few papers on fire. Once the flame burned, he stood up and threw the mattress on the small blaze. "Wanna jump on the mattress till it goes up in flames?" He did not wait for my response; he leapt onto the mattress on the burning pit and began to bounce.

There were tendrils of smoke coming from the bottom of the mattress, and my inner sense of self-preservation cried out to me to say, "No," and walk back home. I could even hear the voice of my mother in my mind say, "Davis, don't you dare!" But I really wanted Jordan to like me. So I jumped on the burning mattress with him. We jumped for what felt like several minutes. It was quite fun. The more we bounced, the safer I began to feel. The freer I began to feel. As the minutes passed, the cloud of smoke around us grew. It started to be hard to see the surrounding area, and the bottoms of my feet grew warm in those brief moments when I landed on the mattress between hops. But we still bounced. That is, until I heard my mother. She was out on our front porch and had spotted us jumping amid rising flames and smoke tendrils.

"DAVIS DANIEL MOORE! GET OVER HERE!" she screamed from the porch.

Jordan and I looked at each other, and we both knew I was dead. My mom is a sweet lady, so when she raises her voice, you know she means business. I was the one in trouble, but we both scattered. Seconds after we hopped off the mattress, the whole thing burst into flames. All at once. The grey fabric of the bed was gone in an instant, wrapped in fiery tongues of flame.

I was grounded that day. I was not allowed to go and hang out with Jordan for a while. I remember getting scolded in the living room by my mother. I do not remember all of the things she said. I remember her talking about how stupid it was to jump on a flaming mattress, and how I could have died, and that if my friends wanted me to jump off a bridge, would I do that too? But my eyes were locked on the burning mattress. We had this big picture window in our living room with full view to our neighbor's fire pit. Smoke filled the Michigan afternoon sky. Flames swirled and danced, consuming everything they touched. The mattress was gone; only a shell of springs and wires remained in the midst of the inferno. And besides thinking about my own mortality and how close I came to being barbecued, I could not get out of my mind the reason I got on the mattress in the first place. I risked my life so someone would like me and not think I was a wimp.

There have been a lot of moments like that in my life, which I look back on and wonder how I could have done something so insane. But if I can be honest, I have always wanted people to approve of me. And I think if a lot of us are honest, most of us have probably been there at some point. Where we step into situations and relationships, not because they are something we want to do, but because we are desperate for the approval of others.

A couple years ago, I was preaching a sermon to our church's youth group about approval. We had been going through a sermon series through the book of First Thessalonians, because the church of Thessalonica was an amazing example of not seeking the approval of those around them but seeking God's approval. To understand the example of the believers in Thessalonica, we have to look at the events that led up to the writing of this letter.

Paul and Silas had come to Thessalonica to preach the gospel. Paul preached in the synagogue and many people became Christians. They started a church. People began to experience the freedom in Jesus. They experienced the broken shackles of their old nature. The shame that had held them no longer had its grip in their life. This attracted other people to start examining the new believer's lives. This inspection caused more people to come to know Jesus. The church was booming.

This made many of the Jewish leaders in the synagogue furious and jealous. So they formed a mob against Paul and Silas (Acts 17). The two men had gone into hiding, and when the mob could not find the church leaders, they grabbed a new believer named Jason and a couple others and carried them into the streets. The authorities took some money from them and let them go quietly. Paul and Silas were able to sneak away into the next town and keep preaching. They faced some harsh persecution after Paul left. We do not know exactly the kind of persecution they went through. But it is bad enough for Paul to write the book of 1 Thessalonians to encourage them to stay strong in the midst of adversity.

So when Paul writes to them after these events, he praises them for their faithfulness in the midst of adversity. Paul praises them because they had so completely and utterly given up the need for the approval of those around them that they had become the outcasts in their society. "We give thanks to God always for all of you, constantly mentioning you in our prayers, remembering before our God and Father your work of faith and labor of love and steadfastness of hope in our Lord Jesus Christ" (1 Thessalonians 1:2-3).

In spite of all of the adversity, they were not shaken. They were not turning away from their faith in Christ. And it would have been easy to do that. A lot of these people had worshipped idols their entire lives. They could have gone back to those idols to fit in with their culture. They could have added Jesus to the list of idols they had worshiped before in order to please the people around them, but they did not. They had experienced true freedom and joy and knew they could never go back.

The crazy thing was, not only were they living out their faith in the midst of difficult circumstances, they were thriving. The church actually spread their faith to the surrounding areas. When I say reaching the surrounding areas, I do not mean giving a tract to the cashier in the town next door when they picked up their groceries. I mean they went from one end of the country to the other, proclaiming this faith the world was trying to destroy. Paul says this about them:

> *For you received the word in much affliction, with the joy of the Holy Spirit, so that you became an example to all the believers in Macedonia and in Achaia. For not only has the word of the Lord sounded forth from you in Macedonia and Achaia, but your faith in God has gone forth everywhere, so that we need not say anything. (1 Thessalonians 1:6-7)*

Macedonia and Achaia were both large provinces in the Roman Empire during Paul's day. Macedonia was the province in which Thessalonica was located. Achaia was to the south. Today Greece, Albania, and North Macedonia make up these areas. So this was not a small sphere of influence but a large region of the world. And the faith of the Thessalonians had stretched from one end of it to the other. Everyone knew that these people were Christians, and it affected everyone in profound ways. The Christians in the other regions were emboldened to live more faithful lives because of the believers in Thessalonica, and non-believers became curious as to how the believers in Thessalonica were able to stand so strong in the midst of such harsh persecution. The pain and adversity the believers went through benefited the people around them. The Christians in Thessalonica allowed themselves to be a beacon of light to the people who were around them, even at great cost to themselves.

Paul goes on to say,

> *For they [those who saw the Thessalonians faith lived out] themselves report concerning us the kind of reception we had among you, and how you turned to God from idols to serve the living and true God, and to wait for his Son from Heaven, whom he raised from the dead, Jesus who delivers us from the wrath to come. (1 Thessalonians 1:9-10)*

They were known for turning their backs on a system of religion that had been practiced for generations to follow this new true God. They were willing to face affliction and not be the most popular people in town so they could worship Jesus. They were willing to face the difficulty, be the social rejects, and lose their property and jobs, all because of Jesus. They were willing to go through the persecution in their city, because they knew no matter what people said about them, no matter what people did to them, their inheritance and identity in Jesus could never be taken away.

These are the things which characterized the church in Thessalonica. This is how people knew them. They were known as the people who had been radically transformed. For the believers in Thessalonica, Christianity was not a belief system they adopted; it was an encounter with a Person who changed them. It did not matter people were against them or did not approve of them; they had met the God of the universe, and they could not back down. They had been made into something brand-new. They no longer needed the approval of others, because the God of the universe, through Jesus, already approved of them.

For many of us, including my ten-year-old self jumping on a flaming mattress, if we want to live in freedom, we must untie the knot of needing the approval of others. Until we can get to a place where we can believe what God thinks about us and rest in His approval He bought for us on the cross, we will strive for the approval of the world. Unfortunately, it is much easier to live for the approval of people who we see on a daily basis than a God we cannot see.

I remember almost a two-year portion of my life where I could not write because of a bad review a friend had given me on a piece of writing I had written. To be honest, I do not remember what he said was awful about it, but the words stuck to me. For two years after his criticism, I would sit down to write and stare at a blinking dot on a screen for hours. His criticism ricocheted around my skull like a wild bullet. There were things I wanted to write, things I needed to write. But they could not escape the bars around my brain and heart. In fact, there was a large stretch of time where the only thing I could write about was the fact I could not write. Even that was deleted when I went to review it the next morning.

I wrote a few pieces during this time, but people would just tell me something was off; I was not writing like I used to. My critic's voice had a grip on my life. I could not let it go.

Every week, I meet with Nick, our discipleship pastor. He is a retired man who is on staff at our church. He disciples us as pastors, making sure we are in a good spot spiritually. Nick is wise; he is one of those people who can see straight to the heart of an issue without a ton of effort. I decided to tell him about my writing issues. I told him the whole story about what had happened and how I could not write. When I finished, he had this knowing smile on his face.

"You gave the authority of your writing away," he said.

"My what?"

"Your commission to write. You gave the authority to your friend, and his approval was more important than God's approval on your work."

I did not say much after that. He was right. I had put my worth as a writer into the hands of someone to whom it did not belong. I was after a person's approval rather than God's. Deep down, I wanted someone to look at my work and say how awesome it was. And when I did not get it, I was crushed. When it came down to it, my identity as a writer was wrapped up in what other people thought of my craft.

But how many things in our life are like that? We become so focused on what other people think of us. We want to impress the boss at work, so we will stay late, neglect our families and personal health, just to gain an employer's approval. Or maybe it is starving ourselves to lose weight in order to be thin enough to be loved. Maybe we come from parents with impossible standards, so we strive for a 4.0 to impress them, to show them we are worthy of their affection. Or maybe we jump on a burning mattress to gain the approval of a friend.

So much of our life is often devoted to trying to gain other people's approval. It is a hamster wheel that never stops spinning. If there is anything I have learned when it comes to living for the approval of other people, it is that no matter how much you strive to please every single person around you, you will never do enough to rest securely. There will always be a nagging feeling in the back of your mind you have to do something more. Living for the approval of other people is a gnawing thought that chews us to the bone.

This is the most beautiful thing about the gospel. The gospel says you do not have to search for your approval from other people anymore. You do not need to be the funny guy, the athletic one, the pretty one, artistic one, the one most likely to succeed, or the driven one anymore. These are all characteristics that could be used to describe part of you, but they are not the essence of you. Christ entered your life and changed and transformed your identity to make you into something brand-new. You no longer have to seek others' approval in order to rest satisfied, because in Christ you have already been approved.

In Christ, we can let go of living for the approval of others. We can get off the hamster wheel of needing to gain the approval of others. At the end of the day, every single person in our lives could reject us; but it does not change the way God feels about us. In fact, Paul says this in the context of servants, but its application stretches to all of us:

> *Bondservants, obey in everything those who are your earthly masters, not by way of eye-service, as people pleasers, but with sincerity of heart, fearing*

> *the Lord. Whatever you do, work heartily, as for the*
> *Lord and not for men, knowing that from the Lord*
> *you will receive the inheritance as your reward.*
> *(Colossians 3:22-24)*

In Christ, we are able to serve other people not in order to gain their approval; rather we are able to serve others because we may live in the identity Christ has given us in the gospel.

We are only able to truly love others when we stop living for their approval. If we live for other's acceptance, we fail to see their true need and pain other than through our kaleidoscope of needing to please them. It is only when we rest in the identity of approval God has given us that we can see one another's needs and truly love one another.

ALTAR CALLS AND BRIMSTONE

Untangling the Knot of Trying to Earn God's Love

When I was growing up in the church, we had weeklong evangelist meetings. The tomato-faced preacher stood on the stage in a dark suit while he yelled at the congregation. He would talk about sin and redemption, hell and punishment, and grace and truth. He did a good job convincing us we were bad people, or at least worse than we thought we were an hour before. Even though he talked about salvation and grace, I usually did not leave with feelings of salvation and grace.

I remember as a young boy responding every night to the altar call, because I realized I had sinned that day and needed to make sure I knew God. I would usually go home afterwards, lay in bed at night, and pray the prayer to invite Jesus into my heart again just to make sure. I was so afraid I had prayed the prayer wrong or did not mean it enough. I was scared some accidental slip of saying the wrong words would bring about my eternal damnation. So I would pray the sinner's prayer again. And again. And again. I may hold a world record for "getting saved" seven times in one day. Nevertheless, no matter what I did, I could not find rest.

For the longest time, I thought my issue was I needed to "mean it enough." Or to believe enough. Or be sincere enough. Or, ultimately, be enough. The reality, though, was that deep down I was still trying to save myself. The bottom line was I believed God was looking at my performance and that performance was going to determine His acceptance of me.

No matter how much I strove, fought, or yearned for the acceptance of God, I could not reach the peace and rest God promises. I would read passages like Romans 8:1-2, which says, "There is therefore now no condemnation for those who are in Christ Jesus. For the law of the Spirit of life has set you free in Christ Jesus from the law of sin and death." I saw passages like Psalm 34:8, which says, "Oh, taste and see that the Lord is good! Blessed is the man who takes refuge in Him!" I longed for the peace and the goodness of God. However, my heart was tumultuous, and I felt like could not enter into that rest.

I could not grasp the idea God would accept me. Maybe He could tolerate me. Perhaps allow me to sit in the corner and watch while He hung out with the really good people. But accepting me as a son who was treasured was a concept that could not compute in my brain. I was stuck in a feedback loop of feeling far from God, praying the sinner's prayer, feeling safe for a couple days before the creeping anxiety stole away my confidence, and then it would start over.

I wish I could say this was a struggle that took me six months and then I got to live in comfort for the rest of my life afterwards. But this was something I would wrestle through for about six years. My life from twelve to eighteen was filled with the back-and-forth seesawing of assurance and doubt. And during this time, I would read books, consult mentors, and pray for clarity. And, time after time, God showed Himself to me. He reminded me I was His child. He would answer my prayers and remind me He was listening. He would convict me of my sin, so I would be led to repentance. He gave me a desire to serve Him with my whole heart. He gave me insight into His Word and led me to application. Time after time, He reminded me I was His child. Through all of this He showed me the issue was deeper than only struggling with my salvation. It was an identity struggle of resting in the fact I was accepted by God. It was in this season God used His Word to cut away at the knot in my life.

Over the years, I have talked with many people who have struggled through this same issue. Just as many of us struggle with the sin issue of needing to win the approval of other people, I think just as many of us struggle trying to earn the acceptance of God.

Many times, when it comes to our core issues, we must often unlearn things before we can learn the truth. Not being able to rest in the acceptance of God is first and foremost an identity issue. Trying to earn God's acceptance is engraved on many of our psyches like initials on trees. And it shows up in our lives in many different forms. For some of us, it is falling into the trap of comparing our conduct with the faith and fervor of other people, whether that comparison makes us look good or bad. *"At least I don't struggle with yelling at my kids like that person does."* Or, *"That person is so much better than me. They always raise their hands in worship, and they are always posting videos of what they are learning from the Bible."*

For others of us, it is putting ourselves through a strict regimen of actions and habits that make us seem spiritual. We stumble around with a list of misplaced priorities, trying to earn something we were never meant to earn. And to answer that identity issue, we must turn to the book of Galatians and learn a quick history lesson.

The book of Galatians was written by Paul to a series of churches throughout the region of Galatia. Paul had previously spent time cultivating the gospel in the churches across this region (found in Acts 13 and 14). The majority of the believers in these churches were Gentiles. Since the Apostle's departure, however, several Christians of the circumcision party (those who insisted on keeping the Old Testament law in addition to the teachings of Jesus), found their way into the church. They insisted these new Galatian Christians must take part in many of the ceremonial aspects of the Jewish faith in order to be "real" Christians. In order to be truly accepted before God, they insisted on adhering to the Jewish feasts and diet restrictions and be circumcised. In short, rather than accepting the free gift of salvation Jesus had purchased for them through the cross, they accepted rules and regulations they had to submit to as additional requirements to experience life in Christ.

Paul wrote the book of Galatians to confront this line of thinking that was warping the theology of the people throughout the region. In the third chapter of the book, he challenged the Galatians:

O foolish Galatians! Who has bewitched you? It was before your eyes that Jesus Christ was publicly portrayed as crucified. Let me ask you this: Did you receive the Spirit by works of the law or by hearing with faith? Are you so foolish? Having begun by the Spirit, are you being perfected by the flesh? Does He

> *who supplies the Spirit to you and works miracles*
> *among you do so by works of the law, or by hearing*
> *with faith? (Galatians 3:1-5)*

Paul challenged their faulty understanding of the gospel by asking a simple question: does your salvation and God's acceptance of you depend on your personal performance or on the sacrifice of Jesus?

While I have never desired to adhere to the Jewish feasts and ceremonial washings so God would love me more, I did feel God was happier with me when I went to church, read the Bible, and prayed. While all of those things are great, beneficial things, none of them add to or subtract from the approval God extends toward us. While God calls us to obedience as we walk with Him, His acceptance of us is based solely on Jesus' work on the cross.

Pastor J.D. Greear wrote a prayer to remind him of the gospel in seasons of difficulty. Part of that prayer applies here. "In Christ, there is nothing I can do that would make You love me more, and nothing I have done that makes You love me less."[13] The bluntness of the gospel is this: we cannot carry ourselves. We cannot rescue ourselves. We cannot earn God's favor. It is a blow to our pride and need for self-sufficiency, but it is the truth.

In fact, Paul makes this blunt claim in Galatians: "We also have believed in Christ Jesus, in order to be justified by faith in Christ and not by works of the law, because by works of the law no one will be justified" (2:16). To have God's acceptance we must first stop trying to earn it. Before we can rest in the approval of God, we must realize we cannot earn God's approval from the start.

That is what makes Christianity so unique from everything else. So many other religions of the world make you grovel at the feet of some deity to earn some semblance of approval—often not knowing if you have done quite enough to ever earn it. Christianity flat out states you or I could never earn God's approval.

Realizing you can never do something can lead to a couple conclusions. The first can be despair. The elderly man or woman looking back on their life and realizing they never had the chance, whether by life's circumstance or volitional choice, to accomplish a life goal or to achieve a childhood dream can be devastating; it can color the life spent with that dark shade we call regret. Or to someone who, due to a horrific accident, will never achieve their life's dream of running a marathon, joining the Navy Seals, or seeing the Great Pyramids of Giza, which can leave them questioning if their new quality of life will be worth living.

In both of these scenarios, or the millions of other scenarios that millions of us experience on a daily basis, where we realize the thing we yearned to achieve is impossible, we find a choice before us. We can despair over what we could not or did not accomplish, or we can lean into how to move forward.

Realizing there is nothing we can do to earn God's approval can be a shot to the heart. All our striving, faithful church attendance, and even myriad attempts at the sinner's prayer do not bring us an inch closer to God. That may be one of the scariest truths to our humanity, especially to the self-sufficient part of us. But in what is meant to be the scariest truth of our humanity, we also see the most beautiful truth. Our approval with God does not rest upon our goodness but in the sacrifice of Jesus. This was the truth I needed to assimilate into my heart.

Finally, somewhere along the line, I stumbled across the book of Hebrews. It was through this text God operated on and healed me. The book of Hebrews is written to an audience wrestling with their faith. They were not resting in the approval of God as they were being persecuted for their faith; they realized it would be easier to go back to Judaism and live under the law. The author writes to beckon them to hold on and hold to the faith they had come to know.

A particular section in Hebrews chapter 9 stood out to me during this season. I know the next section is a little long for a passage to quote. And, if you are like me, it is easy when you are reading a book to skip the large block quotes of Scripture. But this passage became a cornerstone for me; take a second to marinate in it.

> For Christ has entered, not into holy places made
> with hands, which are copies of the true things, but
> into heaven itself, now to appear in the presence of
> God on our behalf. Nor was it to offer himself re-
> peatedly, as the high priest enters the holy places ev-
> ery year with blood not his own. For then he would
> have had to suffer repeatedly since the foundation
> of the world, but as it is, he has appeared once for
> all at the end of the ages to put away sin by the
> sacrifice of himself. And just as it is appointed to
> man to die once, and after that comes judgment, so
> Christ, having been offered once to bear the sins of
> many, will appear a second time, not to deal with
> sin but to save those who are eagerly waiting for
> him. (Hebrews 9:24-28)

This passage hollows me whenever I read it. I see
the priests standing at their duties continually offering
sacrifices to God. I see the blood pouring off the altar
over and over again. When I was eighteen, my parents
moved to Togo, West Africa, to serve as missionaries.
While we lived in Africa, we were invited by a Muslim
friend to go to Tabaski (known as Adha in other parts
of the world), which is an Islamic holiday celebrat-
ing Abraham's willingness to sacrifice Ishmael—or,
in our version of the story, Isaac. There were about
ten thousand Muslims present for the event, and we
were treated as the guests of honor. My family was
brought up in front of the crowd next to a priest and

a goat. Ten thousand sets of eyes looked between us and the priest and the goat. We watched the priest take a knife and gouge a line in the goat's throat as he offered the sacrifice. There was a lot of blood. It cascaded down the blade, hands, and wrists of the priest, and finally onto the ground. It reminded me of the priests in Hebrews. Continually offering animals for sin. Offerings that never ceased, because people always sin. Every day another sacrifice, followed by another and another each day after that.

That is why Jesus came. Not to come every year like the high priest did and continually offer sacrifices for sin. He came not to continue a system of constant bloodshed to cover sin. He came to end it, not with the blood of another animal, but with His own blood.

Another verse in the book of 1 Peter ties in close to our Hebrews passage. "For Christ also suffered once for sins, the righteous for the unrighteous, to bring us to God, being put to death in the flesh but made alive in the spirit" (3:18). Up until this point in human history, to have the approval of God, one had to continually bring a lamb as an offering. But Jesus flipped the script. Approval with God was no longer won through a continual offering of lambs and oxen; it was found in trusting that the sacrifice of Jesus was enough. God's approval was not an award to chase after as much as it was a gift to be received.

It was in these passages I realized I had been fighting the battle over the acceptance of God backwards. Rather than looking at the reality of what Christ had done for me on the cross to influence and motivate my experience, I used my personal experience to determine my reality. I had lived my life up until this moment constantly looking at my interaction with God as the evidence I was accepted.

I realized I had missed the chief assurance of my acceptance by God. It was not found in the fickle state of my emotions and experience. It was looking back at a bloody cross with the final Lamb on it. I had spent so much time trying to make sure I had prayed the prayer right or said the right words, I forgot that the main moment that mattered in the history of my salvation and acceptance had happened two thousand years ago on a hill near Jerusalem. That was the moment the price was paid.

Through Christ's sacrifice we are able to come forward as those called "accepted by God." Not as a people who continually need to offer a sacrifice in order to gain God's love, but as a people who continually point back to Golgotha and say the sacrifice was enough.

WASTING TIME WITH PIT BULLS

Untangling the Knot of Toxic Productivity

Amanda and I have a sixty-pound pit bull/lab mix named Nala. We adopted her from a shelter a few years ago. She is a happy dog with a lot of love to give to the world. But if I am honest, I am not entirely sure the world is ready for her love. She is a spazz, often zipping from one end of the house to the other, spinning in endless circles in search of her tail. Yet, despite her constant stream of energy, she is also probably the most affectionate dog I have ever met. Nala has zero concept of personal space and is usually cuddled up with one of us on the couch. She needs constant companionship to feel safe.

Nala usually sleeps in a crate at the foot of our bed. For the longest time she liked to sleep in for as long as Amanda was asleep. As I am an early riser, she often would see me get out of bed around six, groan, then roll over back to sleep. However, after I was consistently getting out of bed early, I came out of the bathroom one morning to see her whimpering in her crate, forehand pressed against the onyx bars, looking at me with those giant brown eyes. I let her out and took her outside to do her business. Then I fed her while I made my coffee. I brought my coffee to my office where I meet with God. Nala brought her bone and joined me.

She laid on my lap while I read and prayed. (Nala believes she is a lap dog.) After my time in the Scriptures, I moved over to my desk to write. I got about fifteen minutes in when Nala came back into the room with her toy rope and laid it in my lap. She loves tug-of-war. She whined and nudged the rope closer to me. I sighed and picked up one end of the rope. She grabbed the other and tugged hard. I gave it a couple shakes, then threw it so she could chase it. Then I returned to work.

I had only plunked a few keys when she brought it back and laid it in my lap. I felt a spark of frustration, because this was the one time during the day I have set aside to write. I shoved her away and kept on typing. She sat, then growled, a low rumbling growl she uses when she beckons for my attention. She picked up the rope and laid it in my lap again. I played for a few more seconds and threw it out of the room and quickly shut the door. Quiet. A few minutes later, a light whimper came from the other side of the door. Then suddenly, a dark snout pushed underneath the space at the bottom of the door into my office. And a single, blinking brown eye stared back at me.

This memory reminds me I am often obsessed with productivity. My wife makes fun of me because almost everything I do has to have some productive value to it. If I am mowing the lawn, running, driving, or doing the dishes, I use the time to listen to a podcast or a book. A large part of my identity has always been accomplishing a goal.

We live in a breakneck culture obsessed with accomplishment. We have this American dream mindset that tells us if we put our mind to it and hustle, we can attain anything we desire. And while we are blessed to live in a land where there is freedom and choice to be able to chase dreams, the culture surrounding this becomes toxic to a biblically centered life. This culture tells us if we are not accomplishing the goals we have set for ourselves, we are either not doing enough to reach those goals, or we are not willing to put everything on the line to reach them.

In our culture, we worship the idea of being ultra-productive. We have entire blogs and internet content creators devoted to maximizing our productivity, pushing us to the maximum output. With the modern age of smart phones, we can often work on the go. Whether we leave the office or not, we are reachable and often expected to be at the ready to work more and perform more. We are always on the go. Always producing, always crafting, always putting in the hours, building these sandcastles around ourselves in hope of resting satisfied.

Have we ever stopped to ask ourselves why we feel like we have to accomplish all of these goals? Why do we feel like we will finally feel at rest only when we finish our endeavors? When I graduated college, or ran my first 5k, or finished the first draft of my first novel, I felt elated. I felt like I had completed the most important thing in my life. Until the next day. Then there was a new goal, a new quest, and new mission I needed to conquer. How much of our lives do we spend chasing our goals thinking they are the things that are going to satisfy us and finally let us rest?

For many of us, there is a sinking fear when we sit down at the end of the day to enjoy an episode of TV with our family, or curl up on the couch with a good book, or even play tug-of-war with the dog that we are wasting time. We may worry that the sands of time are slipping through our fingertips, and we are wasting it. Many of us have fused our hustle to our identity, which causes our worth to become knotted up with the things we produce. The truth is, our slavery to the hustle is a signifier of a deeper issue.

We are not the only ones who get caught up in the grind. King Solomon did too. Solomon inherited the throne after his father, King David. When he took the throne, he made sure business got done. He is known for having completed the great temple of God overlaid in pure gold (1 Kings 5:6). He is known for collecting and arranging thousands of proverbs and psalms for Israeli worship (Proverbs 1:1-5) and building a gilded army with 1,400 chariots and 12,000 horsemen (1 Kings 10:26). He cultivated diplomatic relationships with many of the countries around him, marrying several of the other kings' daughters to make peaceful relations with their nations, and established and developed successful trade links with many nations across the seas to create a fast flowing economy. To top it all off, he was also so wise, people would come from all over the world to inquire of his wisdom and what they should do with their various problems. Solomon's productivity levels would put all of us to shame.

Because of his wisdom, he is often credited for writing the book of Ecclesiastes. It is a blunt, honest look at our humanity and what is truly important. Solomon, or "The Teacher" as he refers to himself, writes this book at the end of his life. He reflects on all of his accomplishments, and the fruits of his labor he spent so much time constructing. Much of the book is a lament, because as he looks at all he had accomplished and the kingdom he had constructed, he says, "I have seen everything that is done under the sun, and behold, all is vanity and a striving after wind" (Ecclesiastes 1:14). The phrase, "under the sun" is an image he repeats over and over again to represent anything that we do to live for the things of the world. He says that living for the things of the world is like chasing the wind.

Later in the book, he says, "What has a man from all the toil and striving of heart with which he toils beneath the sun? For all his days are full of sorrow, and his work is a vexation. Even in the night his heart does not rest. This also is vanity" (Ecclesiastes 2:22-23). When we spend all our days under the sun working, striving, and hustling for our personal goals, to the point we cannot sleep at night or enjoy the people God has placed into our lives because we cannot scrape our goals from our minds, the writer says that life is worthless.

The goals we set on this earth will all one day turn to dust. Our construction and great architecture will one day fall apart, our books will be forgotten, our currency will burn, our chiseled social media image will one day disappear, and people will forget us. One of the whole points of the book of Ecclesiastes is that life on Earth is empty when lived for the things on Earth. It is ironic: the meaning we seek to find in the work and productivity itself turns out to be meaningless if it is the focus.

But it is not only the personal dreams we chase that cause us to miss the point. I have found toxic productivity often can creep into ministry. Pastoring is a tenuous job. It is not linear like most nine-to-fives, where you go in, have a set task list, and go home at the end of the day. There are often days when people call and need to meet and talk through heartbreaks and emotional explosions, or there is a meeting that will go far beyond the allotted time. The other part of ministry is the work is never done. You could wake up and start working at 6:00 a.m. and never stop, because there is always something to be doing. Whether it is ministering to people directly, writing sermons, planning meetings, seeking vision, or researching culture, theology, or counseling methods, the work never ceases. I remember when I first entered pastoral ministry; I would often work ten to twelve hours most days because it did not seem like there was an end to the work. It was easy to get swept up in doing things for God and miss out on what God was trying to communicate in the midst of it.

Jesus talked about people who will work for God and even be productive. He said:

> *"Not everyone who says to me, 'Lord, Lord,' will enter the kingdom of heaven, but the one who does the will of my Father who is in heaven. On that day many will say to me, 'Lord, Lord, did we not prophesy in your name, and cast out demons in your*

> *name, and do many mighty works in your name?'*
> *And then will I declare to them, 'I never knew*
> *you; depart from me, you workers of lawlessness.'"*
> *(Matthew 7:21-23)*

The people Jesus talked about here are the most productive of any of us. I would consider casting out demons and doing miracles as a little more productive—at least in a theatrical sense—than stacking chairs after the church potluck. And these people, when they get to the judgment seat, will bring the amazing things they did for God and show Jesus their ministry portfolio like they are interviewing for a job impressing the new boss. And Jesus will say to them, "Depart from me, I never knew you." This passage is hollowing. Fruit in ministry is important, and God often calls us to accomplish great things for Him. But if in our work or ministry we miss the call of the Creator of the universe, we have missed the boat.

When the drive running our life comes in the form of toxic productivity, it is often based on the desire of trying to prove or present ourselves as "enough," whether that is to parents, God, friends, spouses, bosses, or even ourselves. We have this need to prove ourselves as someone who was worthy. Worthy of love, affection, honor, praise, and worth. We cannot often persuade our tired hearts that God does not see us through that lens. We forget the identity Christ gave us on the cross, which says we no longer need to prove ourselves to be accepted, but through the cross we are already accepted. We often take the perspective of the world's system of religion, which talks about doing and doing and doing in order to be accepted.

I remember visiting a friend in China when I was in high school. We went to a Buddhist temple, and there were crowds of people bowing to a multitude of deities. We saw this one woman smashing her face into the pavement as she bowed over and over again. When she came up there were flecks of blood on her forehead. I asked my friend's parents why she would do something like that. They said she believed the lower and harder she bowed, the more her god would see her as sincere. Many times, we are just like her. We somehow believe our commitment to the hustle proves our worth before God and others.

Rich, a pastor friend of mine, often talks about the importance of doing things with God rather than for God. I once asked him what he meant. He told me we love the idea of being the hero, being the guy who goes out and does all the work and gets the credit. He told me our lives are ultimately about joining in with God in the grand story He is telling and accomplishing tasks as we are sent. We are not the hero of the story God is telling, but the sidekick. The tasks we do for Him are not done in a sense to gain His approval or love; they are done out of the love and gratitude we have for Him. In the midst of our productivity of doing things *for* God, we cannot forget to *be* with God.

The most famous passage in the Bible that illustrates productivity and being is found in Luke chapter 10.

> *Now as they went on their way, Jesus entered a village. And a woman named Martha welcomed him into her house. And she had a sister called Mary, who sat at the Lord's feet and listened to his teaching. But Martha was distracted with much serving. And she went up to him and said, "Lord, do you not care that my sister has left me to serve alone? Tell her then to help me." But the Lord answered her, "Martha, Martha, you are anxious and troubled about many things, but one thing is necessary. Mary has chosen the good portion, which will not be taken away from her." (10:38-42)*

In this passage, we see two distinct postures of the heart. Mary sat at the feet of Jesus to learn from Him. Martha got distracted in her serving of Him. Mary was captured by Christ. Martha was captured by doing things for Christ. Mary's heart was consumed toward Jesus. Martha was consumed with resentment toward Mary. And when she looked at all the preparation needed for Jesus' hospitality, she complained about her sister to Jesus.

Jesus' response is so interesting: "Martha, Martha, you are anxious and troubled about many things, but one thing in necessary. Mary has chosen the good portion, which will not be taken away from her" (Luke 10:41-42). The issue with Martha was not that she was busy preparing food for the guests, cleaning the dishes, or making sure everyone's drinks were topped off. In the midst of the work, she missed the Creator of the universe beckoning her to come near and be at rest.

Rest in Scripture is not necessarily about ceasing work. But it does change the perspective and posture upon which the work is done. Work done from a heart at rest does not seek to prove oneself to God or others. In fact, it does just the opposite.

Jesus says, "Come to me all who labor and are heavy laden. And I will give you rest" (Matthew 11:28). The prerequisite to coming and receiving rest is admitting we are heavy laden. It is the acknowledgment before God that our striving and laboring does not prove ourselves to anyone.

To be able to do things with God instead of for God is a vulnerable posture. We have to let go of our grip on the story that God needs us. To untie the knot of toxic productivity we must come to terms with the fact God does not need us, but He does want us.

He invites us to step into the story with Him. Life is a gift. We only get it for as long as He gives it. We did not choose to have breath breathed through our nostrils. God did. He does not make mistakes. Just as Jesus called to the fishermen on the Sea of Galilee, and just as He called to Martha in the midst of her frustration, He calls to us in the midst of our hurry to get things done.

All our striving and stress is unneeded and counter to what God desires for us. I love watching the seasons change and how they arrive each year in their time without my willing so or not. The leaves still fall every year, and the trees still bud in the spring. There is a time and season for all things. If we were to turn back to Ecclesiastes, we would find Solomon say in the midst of his lament, "I have seen the burden God has laid on the human race. He has made everything beautiful in its time" (3:9-11). It is a comfort to know God makes everything beautiful in its time. In the passage preceding this one, Solomon says there is a time for everything under heaven. Whether being born, dying, weeping, laughing, mourning, dancing, embracing, gaining, losing, tearing, sewing, speaking, or keeping silence, there is a time and a season for all things.

The same is true in our lives. There is a time to be productive. To hit the grind and be faithful in our careers, to make our kid's sack lunch before they go to school in the morning, and to serve faithfully alongside our brothers and sisters in the local church. There is a time for worship, like Mary, where we withdraw and spend time with God, studying His Word and taking time to appreciate Him for who He is. And there is a time for rest, where we take a nap, take a walk outside, and maybe even waste time with a pit bull who just wants to play tug-of-war.

The teacher in Ecclesiastes says there is nothing better than for people to be happy with the work God has given them to do—not to live for the work, but to enter into the work with a grateful and happy heart. Realizing we are no longer trying to prove ourselves, but to thrive in the work He has placed for us to do. This work is not done in an effort to gain favor from anyone, but from the overflow of a grateful heart for the favor God has already bestowed on us.

THE EXTRAORDINARY ORDINARY

Untangling the Knot of Needing to be Somebody

When I was young, I thought I wanted to be a rockstar. I watched 80's music videos with my dad, with the big-haired men jumping all around the stage while they strummed guitars. They looked like they were living life to the fullest. I was in awe at how the crowd would roar between songs as something the band said resonated with them. It was not until later in my life that I realized all I truly wanted from that dream was to be known and understood.

Sometimes our sin nature seizes our deepest long- ings and knots them into things we never intended them to become. I think all of us deep down are seek- ing to be understood and known. We desire to have relationships in which we can be vulnerable and real, where people can see the ugliness of our hearts and not run away. However, because of our insecurity, we twist this God-given desire of connection from longing to be known, to *needing* to be someone. Rather than chasing after the intimacy vulnerability brings, we would rather chase the cheap knockoff of sentimen- tal popularity. This is the piece God wishes to unknot from our identity.

In our last chapter, we talked about how a God-giv- en drive to produce can sometimes transform into toxic productivity. We talked about how our culture praises those who commit to the hustle and create a sculpted personal kingdom. However, I think there is another message our culture whispers in our blood. We are told if we want to live a worthwhile and satisfy- ing life, we must push past the ordinary and step into the extraordinary.

Our society, by and large, is highly individualis- tic. We do not often look at ourselves as a piece of a much larger collective organism; rather, we look at ourselves as the main character in our own personal stories. These are stories where our dreams are the ultimate quests we seek to accomplish.

In our culture, we are told to go out and do something extraordinary. We are told to have big dreams, to go and do something radical, to leave a legacy and make a difference. We give Dr. Seuss' *Oh, the Places You Will Go* to our graduating seniors, sending them off into the world with messages like, "Kid, you'll move mountains! You're off to great places. Today is your day! Your mountain is waiting. So…get on your way!"[14] We send our students off into the world with visions of an extraordinary destiny filled with power and promises of becoming anything they wish to become.

While, inevitably, there will be those in those graduating classes who will go on to change the way we look at medicine, art, literature, or infrastructure, the truth is—whether we would like to admit this or not—most of us will not go on to do extraordinary things that change the course of history. Chances are, we will not become the president of the United States. Most of us will not be the next Shakespeare. Most of us will not find the cure for cancer.

Most of us will live "ordinary" lives. Maybe as you read that sentence, there was a negative, knee-jerk reaction to the word "ordinary." I think, for many of us, the word "ordinary" tastes like a swig of day-old coffee left on our end table from the night before. "Ordinary" does not stand out in the crowd; it does not have flashing lights dancing around it. It is just "ordinary." We live in a culture that elevates the movie star,

NFL player, and social media influencer but is silent about the wonders of the stay-at-home mom, factory worker, or elementary teacher. Our culture elevates the extraordinary as the ideal and fears the reality of the ordinary.

As I was doing research for this chapter, I did a quick Google search of "ordinary vs. extraordinary." I found plenty of blog posts and articles explaining how to go from an ordinary life to an extraordinary one. How to lay hold of the dream and be a person who is interesting, successful, and always gets the girl. "Ordinary" in these articles was someone who was missing out on their full potential. "Ordinary" people in these articles were seen as the lazy and dull.

I believe we are petrified of being seen as uninteresting and dull. In fact, most of our social media culture is wrapped around the idea of making our lives seem more exciting. We post the exciting pieces of our lives, the pieces that make us seem interesting and set apart from the crowd. We are fueled to do so by the billions of other interesting shards of people's lives uploaded into the ether every single day. We have to be honest about what they are: highlight reels. What we see on social media is not our real lives. They are shards, mere pieces of our lives. The pieces we are okay with other people seeing. We think if we can get others to believe our lives are exciting and extraordinary, then maybe we can believe it too.

Our Instagram culture is built around covering the fact we are ordinary people living ordinary lives. Our sewn-together social identity is often formed to cover the nakedness of our own insecurity. In America, we live in the culture of the "land of opportunity." We believe if we work long enough and commit to the hustle, then anything we put our minds to is possible. The thing of it is, oftentimes, this can be true. To accomplish our goals, we often have to buckle down, have some grit, and go to work. Chasing dreams often means waking up an hour before work, in the wee hours of the morning, to work on that project, train for the marathon, paint the sunrise, or whatever shape our extraordinary dreams take. And it is all well and good. But in the chase of our extraordinary dreams of what life could be like, are we missing out on the ordinary moments where life and God intersect?

Some of these dreams are cheap imitations of our base desire to know what it means to be human. Most of us would say we want our lives to count and to leave a legacy that will echo past our days. I believe this a God-given drive. It is our sin nature that twists and turns our dreams into a selfish desire to be important and be someone who garners the attention of other people. Our sin nature woos and convinces us that we must become something.

If anyone deserved praise and admiration, it was Jesus. If there was anyone who deserved everyone to be constantly bowing at His feet and following Him on social media, it was Jesus. However, when we see Jesus, we often see Him serving, rather than being served. The God of the universe, the One who crafted stars and galaxies, mountains and rivers, atoms and physics, bent down to serve His creation. To be honest, there is not much extraordinary (in the worldly sense) about that. This was nothing but sheer humility. Jesus did not even have a social media account filled with posts about all His service projects that He did.

As a culture, we need a better definition of the word "ordinary." In our society, when we hear the word "ordinary," we have several stereotypes pop in our minds: boring, routine, typical, lazy, or dry, to name a few. "Ordinary" does not stand out in a crowd, it does not become a social media influencer, and it does not have its name in lights; it is not extravagant. Most of us spend most of our lives trying to escape the "ordinary."

The reality is God often calls us into something deeper than the small identities we come up with for ourselves. Michael Horton, in his book titled *Ordinary*, talks about how a major part of our cultural issue is we miss the true source of our identity.

> *Because rather than seeing ourselves as self-creators who choose our own identity and purpose, the biblical worldview tells us that we are on the receiving end of our existence. We are beholden to*

someone else. Our life is a gift from God, not our own achievement. And our ingratitude is the clearest expression that we have idolized ourselves."[15]

In seeking our dreams, we often reveal we idolize ourselves.

In the Gospel of Matthew chapter 20, a few of the disciples got into an argument about who was the greatest among them. James and John's mother even weighed in and requested Jesus let her sons sit on Jesus' right and left hand in the new kingdom. The disciples viewed their following of Jesus as a springboard into greatness, power, and fame. Jesus quickly responded to this line of thinking among His followers:

You know that the rulers of the Gentiles lord it over them, and their great ones exercise authority over them. It shall not be so among you. But whoever would be great among you must be your servant. And whoever would be first among you must be your slave, even as the Son of Man came not to be served but to serve, and to give his life as a ransom for many. (Matthew 20:25-28)

Rather than bolstering His disciples' drive to be extraordinary and the front of the pack, He told them the greatest in the kingdom of God would be the least in the eyes of the world. And Jesus did not say this to hoard all the popularity and splendor to Himself; He lived what He preached. In fact, flip a few pages over, and we see Jesus washing the feet of His disciples. Foot washing in Jesus' day was not something the master of a house did. It was something a servant did. Yet we see Jesus bending to do the work of a servant.

Right after graduating from college, I got an internship at the church where I now pastor. One day, the pastor I interned under asked me to show up to our staff meeting half an hour early to help him with a project. I showed up to find him unstacking chairs in the sanctuary. He said, "If you ever come to a point in your ministry that anything short of holding a microphone is beneath you, you do not deserve the microphone."

The truth is, we have even made an extraordinary thing out of Christian service. Social media reels are filled with photos of missions trips to Mexico where people pose with orphans in ratty clothes. They are usually captioned with, "So blessed to be able to be in Guadalajara, Mexico, helping this orphanage. I expected to be a blessing to others—I didn't expect to be the one who got blessed." There is usually an airplane emoji too. These missions *experiences* become the thing to be chased after, rather than the *people* they are meant to be for. They become a place for personal revelation and reflection rather than serving others. And, yes, God often can use these types of trips to reveal things in our lives and even teach us great things about Him. And, yes, in serving others, we ourselves can be blessed. But when the trips we take under the guise of "serving others" becomes about the stuff we are getting out of it, we prove we care more about our own image and story than serving others.

When Jesus was getting ready to leave earth, He left his disciples with a last command:

> *"All authority in heaven and on earth has been given to me. Go therefore and make disciples of all nations, baptizing them in the name of the Father and of the Son and of the Holy Spirit, teaching them to observe all that I have commanded you. And behold, I am with you always, even to the end of the age." (Matthew 28:18-20)*

The word "Go" here is interesting. Many times when I have heard it preached, the pastor uses this as a call for global missions. We should drop everything we have and join the two-week trip to Mexico. While there certainly can be an inclusion of global missions in this passage, it is not the immediate context of what Jesus is getting at. The word "Go" here is referring to something slightly different. It is better translated, "As you go." Meaning, as you live your life. As you go to the store because you are out of groceries. As you pass in the hallways between Algebra II and British Literature. As you sit in the waiting room at the dentist office waiting for the receptionist to call you forward. As you go to soccer practice. It is a call to carry Jesus in the midst of ordinary moments. Every ordinary opportunity of normal life is a call to take up the cross and follow after Christ and take His love with you. You do not need to take a trip overseas to carry your faith.

In fact, if you are not doing it while you go about your daily life, you probably are not going to effectively do it overseas either. When we forget to live our faith in the ordinary moments, we show we are not ready for the extraordinary. The truth is, we will not be able to embrace the Great Commission in its fullest context until we take our blinders off that look for the extraordinary and we live in the ordinary.

In our last chapter, we talked about Solomon as the definition of productivity. But in the book of Ecclesiastes, we see he was also the definition of what we would call extraordinary. For those who desire riches, he had more money than most of us combined will ever possess. He ran out of stuff to do with his gold. He built gardens and wonders and had everything a person could ever desire. For those who love pleasure, this guy lived the utmost of luxury. He even says he kept nothing from himself. If he wanted it, he got it. He is known for having three hundred wives and seven hundred concubines. Also, he was known as the wisest man in the world. People from all over the world would come to hear his wisdom.

In essence, Solomon was Steve Jobs, Hugh Hefner, and Tony Stark all jammed into one guy (minus the Iron Man suit). However, when he got to the end of chasing his extraordinary life, he realized the whole thing was empty and a striving for the wind. In fact, after chasing the extraordinary, he said, "Then I considered all that my hands had done and the toil I had expended in doing it, and behold, all was vanity and a striving after wind, and there was nothing to be gained under the sun" (Ecclesiastes 2:11). The whole thing was empty.

The power to send armies to neighboring kingdoms and gain land. *Empty.* The Coachella-level parties featuring his name as the sponsor. *Empty.* The endless stream of women and sensual pleasure. *Empty.* Bathing in the riches of his toil. *Empty.* His vast influence, causing neighboring dignitaries to come listen to his wisdom and intelligence. *Empty.* In the end, he discovered all his influence and power and gross personal income was naught but two fists grasping at the wind. The dream of extraordinary, it seems, did not keep its promise.

What is interesting, however, was that as he pulled everything in the garage of his life out into the driveway, he discovered something. Solomon says, "There is nothing better for a person than that he should eat and drink and find enjoyment in his toil. This also, I saw, is from the hand of God," (Ecclesiastes 2:24). Joy, he found, did not come from the achieving of dreams and accomplishing. It did not come from gaining influence or followers, but in the ordinary. In the waking up to the blare of the alarm clock, to go to the same shop you have worked at for the last twenty years. It is found in the raising of children. It is found in the going to class and cramming for finals. Joy and success is not measured by the depth of your pocket-book or the height of fame or how many social media followers you have; it is found in the contentment of where God has placed you, blooming in the soil of the ordinary.

There is something beautiful about the ordinary. This is not to say that I do not love the experiences of the exotic. I have walked the Great Wall of China (or a piece of it anyway) and entered the vast rooms of the Forbidden City (or at least a few of them). I have haggled prices for goods in African markets in a foreign language. I have slept on airport couches while I held onto my luggage because we were in a shady airport. I bounced in the bed of a pickup truck as we chased after lions in the African wilderness. I have had plenty of extraordinary experiences that became treasured memories. I hope to have many more.

However, there is something beautiful about the ordinary, pushing past the idealistic concepts of what we wish things could be like to live in the actual moments in which we live. I used to idealize writing. I would picture myself writing in dimly lit coffee shops sipping on a latte while I people-watched and wrote down concepts for which Thoreau would give me a fist bump.

Often, reality is much different. Currently, I am seated in my home office with a blanket draped over my lap. There are ringed coffee stains all over the top of my desk. I hear the soft snores of Nala in the giant, oversized chair behind me. On the floor around me are chewed-up tennis balls and a gnawed bone. Nala will alternate between short naps and chewing vigorously on her toys. As I write, I often hit the backspace more than I write forward. I feel like most of what I say is derivative, and I wonder if anyone will benefit from of it. Sometimes, I feel like I spend most of the time flipping through social media. The concepts I write down definitely are not worthy of Thoreau. He would probably look down, yawn, and talk about how he wants to go back to his pond. Then I wonder why I care about his opinion; we disagree on most things anyway.

The problem is not our dreams and aspirations; it is the role they play in our hearts. How much of your identity is wrapped up in your personal visions of success? If God were to come to you and ask you to be a factory worker for the rest of your life, would you feel like you were wasting your life? Or would you lay hold of the quest God had assigned to you and say, "Yes, Lord."

The measure of greatness in someone's life has nothing to do with how many books they wrote, how many companies they started, or how many marathons they ran. The measure of greatness in a life is determined by a life that has been submitted to Christ's call on them. For some it will look like going on to start a very successful company. Others write great books that influence culture. Some will be politicians. Some will be stay-at-home moms raising kids from the crack of dawn till nightfall (and sometimes beyond). Some will work in factories. Some will be elementary school teachers. Some will own a small family business. Some will clean houses. Greatness is defined as the submission to the call Christ has on each and every one of us.

Ambition then, is not so much a virtue as it is a vice. In our individualistic culture, we see that our ambitions provide the lines of color that shape us as unique. C.S. Lewis once said this in reference to our continual dying to self to find our true identity in Christ, but I think it applies here in our searching of needing to be extraordinary.

> *Give up yourself, and you will find your real self. Lose your life and you will save it. Submit to death, including the death of your ambitions, favorite wishes every day, and even the death of your whole body in the end. Submit with every fiber of your being, and you will find eternal life. Keep back nothing. Nothing that you have not given away will be really yours. Nothing in you that has not died will ever be raised from the dead. Look for yourself, and you will find in the long run only hatred, loneliness,*

despair, rage, ruin, and decay. Look for Christ, and you will find Him and with Him everything else thrown in.[16]

At the death of our ambition and desire to be something great or unique, we truly find greatness, uniqueness, and true ambition. We even find a sense of contentment in where we have been placed. We find extraordinary was not what we once expected it to be; we find it looks much more ordinary than we thought.

CHAPTER 13

JESUS WRAPPED IN RED, WHITE, AND BLUE

Untangling the Knot of Idolizing One's Culture

When I was a teenager, I had a T-shirt that said "JesUSAves." It was colored red, white, and blue and sported American stripes and a couple stars underneath it. I think it illustrates a common issue facing the Church. The message of the shirt—at least on the surface—is innocent. "Jesus Saves." It is a great message. It is the mantra to which I have given my entire life. The USA at the center of the shirt, however, reflects a cultural identity to which much of the American Church has given itself. Country first and Jesus wrapped around it like cellophane. I always found it interesting the "Jesus saves" on the shirt was in lowercase, with small letters in the background, while USA was front and center, bolded—large and in charge. A veneer of Christianity surrounding a beating heart of a flag.

I was talking with a friend the other day. He is a youth pastor at a church down the road. We usually meet up once a month or so and talk about ministry or church life in general. During our last meeting, we talked about how the lines of faith in Jesus and America have a tendency to become blurred, and we talked about how to communicate and address this systemic issue in the Church. My friend said it was hard to address the issue without stepping on toes. I agreed. In our country, freedom, flags, abortion, second amendment, immigration, president, troops, are all charged words with the possibility to cause emotional responses in us, both positive and negative.

A lot of times, when we talk about issues in our nation, it can come across like we are ungrateful or not thankful for the real sacrifices made by real people to maintain the freedoms we enjoy on a daily basis. These challenges and miscommunications, however, do not negate the need for the conversations to take place. For the conversations to be successful, we as the Church must come to the table with hearts willing to show grace and humility, wiling to have our toes stepped on in order for real change and real unity to take place.

For many of us, we have a tendency to view ourselves as citizens of America first and then citizens of the kingdom of God. I do not think many of us would admit this. We may say we are Christians first then citizens of the United States second; however, for many Christians, our actions say otherwise. We often blur the lines between being a citizen of our country and being a citizen of the kingdom of God. We often treat the United States as the kingdom of God, rather than actually taking part in the kingdom that Christ is building in us and through us regardless of where we physically live.

We live in a politically polarized age. Our culture likes to point fingers at the other side of the aisle. The Left takes shots at the Right. The Right blames the Left for the issues happening. Any sort of formal discourse to work through these issues usually devolves into caricatured arguments with unseen commentators on social media. American politics today can tend to often look more like an old western film's barroom brawl than a system that seeks to act for the betterment of the people. And those of us in the Church are often caught up in the fray as much as those outside the Church.

There is nothing wrong about being passionate about what is going on in our country. Being informed is an important piece of being engaged with the world in which we live. But when our passion for politics causes us to hate those on the other side of the aisle, to strip them of their humanness and innate value as an image bearer of God, we have made our American identity and our own opinions into idols. If we get more fired up about who is sitting in the White House rather than the gospel and the fact God wants to communicate His love through us, then we have placed our identity in our earthly country, not our heavenly one.

In the book of Matthew, Jesus made a poignant claim: "No one can serve two masters, for either he will hate the one and love the other, or he will be devoted to the one and despise the other. You cannot serve God and money" (6:24). In context, Jesus was talking about the importance of where we place our treasure. Whether we spend our time collecting the things of this world, which rot and perish, or whether we value the things that truly matter. Jesus went so far to say, "Where your treasure is, there your heart will be also" (Matthew 6:21). This does not only apply to possessions or pursuit of fame; it applies to our citizenship as well. If our treasure is our political leanings, like who is in power or what bills are passed or what freedoms are preserved, we are placing our treasure in things that will rot.

We have a tendency to twist Jesus and Uncle Sam until all we see is a bleached-out Middle Eastern man wrapped in an American flag. We have twisted our faith and our country in such a knot, I am afraid there are many well-meaning people caught worshipping a false god. I think if many Christians were honest, we are much more passionate about America being first in the world's scene than the kingdom God is building. Jesus' motto is not "America first." It is "My kingdom come, my will be done, on earth as it is in heaven."

But it is not only an overzealous idolatry of our country that takes place. There is a movement in the Church today that promotes a harsh isolation from what is happening in the world. It is often justified with Scripture verses like this: "Dear friends, I urge you as foreigners and temporary residents to abstain from fleshly desires which wage war against your soul" (1 Peter 2:11). This passage labels us as pilgrims longing for the kingdom of God. There are many well-meaning Christian, frustrated and fearful of the trajectory of culture at large, who disengage and withdraw from society. I have spoken with a lot of Christians who want to disengage from caring about the needs in our culture, because it is a "lost cause." I have even spoke to Christians who have gone to the extent of saying we should retreat to the homestead and just wait for Jesus to come back. The problem with this line of thinking is it is a divine escapism leading us to reject our responsibility as Christians to be a salt and a light in our current cultural context (Matthew 5:13-16).

We are called to engage people with the love of Christ—not only with the side of the political aisle we agree with the closest, but with *all* people. As Christians, we must be engaged with our culture, and the people in it, as agents of change. In the midst of being a citizen of the United States, Jesus calls us to live and find our identity as a citizen of the kingdom of God.

Jesus' famous sermon, the Sermon on the Mount, found in the early parts of the Gospel of Matthew, in many ways is about the misunderstanding of kingdom. The word "kingdom" for the Jewish people was a charged word. When they thought of the word kingdom, they did not think about what we think about. They did not think of castles or knights or treasure. It was not a word filled with a reminiscing of ancient or medieval times; it was a word that filled them with longing.

They would have thought about the land God had promised to them through their father Abraham. They would have thought about their ancestors enslaved in Egypt and the longing to be set free. This would have reminded them of God breaking Pharaoh through rivers of blood and the death of the firstborn. The people of Israel would have remembered the exodus, Moses parting the Red Sea, and Joshua's leadership as they conquered the promised land. Everything was at peace for a while as they lived in the promise and prosperity of God. However, the Israelites were a rebellious people. They did not stay true to God. They worshiped false idols and did not listen to God's pleas of fidelity, which brought judgment. The Babylonians led them into exile, and there is a sense where the people felt like that they had fallen all the way back to Egypt. God's people were then passed from abusive owner to abusive owner as Persia took over the Babylonians and then the Greeks took over the Persians. Once again there was a longing for kingdom.

Around 167 BC, the Jewish Maccabees led a revolt to overthrow their dictators, and they enjoyed a measure of success. They regained a sense of the "kingdom" for which they longed. It was short-lived, however. About a hundred years later, in 63 BC, the Romans took over.

Nevertheless, many scholars estimate during the Maccabean revolt that the Israelite's sense of kingdom evolved. They began to see their future Messiah as a military leader who would lead them from bondage to political freedom. It became the highest ideal when the Romans came in and took over. In fact, it began to change their understanding of Scripture. When they looked back on all the passages and prophecies talking about a coming Messiah who would set them free, they began to picture a messiah who would free them from the Romans rather than their sin. Rather than seeking a spiritual salvation, they looked for a ruler who would make them politically liberated and restore the sense of kingdom they lost.

Kingdom, in a sense, became a buzzword. So, when Jesus started talking about the "kingdom," people took notice.

> *And he went throughout all Galilee, teaching in their synagogues and proclaiming the gospel of the kingdom and healing every disease and every affliction among the people. So his fame spread throughout all Syria, and they brought him all the sick, those afflicted with various diseases and pains, those oppressed by demons, those having seizures, and paralytics, and he healed them. And great crowds followed him from Galilee and the Decapolis, and from Jerusalem and Judea, and from beyond the Jordan. (Matthew 4:23-25)*

Jesus started going around and preaching about the kingdom and curing diseases at the same time. He spoke to the culture and backed up His preaching with signs and wonders. Kingdom, it seems, attracted the attention of the people. Crowds gathered to see if their Savior had come.

Consequently, in the next chapter, when the crowds were gathered to hear Jesus' famous Sermon on the Mount, I can picture Jesus looking over this crowd of faces, every eyeball trained on Him as He sat down to teach. Assembled before Him were the religious, the hungry, the self-righteous, the poor, the rich, the saintly, and the pagan. You can hear the pause of tense, silent anticipation in the second between He parted His lips to speak the first syllables, paired with the sound of the drumbeat of a million synchronized eyelids, blinking as they waited for Jesus words.

And he opened his mouth and taught them, saying: "Blessed are the poor in spirit for theirs is the kingdom of heaven. Blessed are those who mourn, for they shall be comforted. Blessed are the meek, for they shall inherit the earth. Blessed are those who hunger and thirst for righteousness, for they shall be satisfied. Blessed are the merciful, for they shall receive mercy. Blessed are the pure in heart, for they shall see God. Blessed are the peacemakers, for they shall be called sons of God. Blessed are those who are persecuted for righteousness sake, for theirs is the kingdom of heaven. Blessed are you when others revile you and persecute you and utter all kinds of evil against you falsely on my account. Rejoice and be glad, for your reward is great in heaven, for so they persecuted the prophets who were before you." (Matthew 5:2-12)

I picture there was a stunned silence and a few hanging jaws as Jesus finished speaking. The kingdom that Jesus began to paint before them was not the kingdom the people expected and longed for. It was not a militarized state where the heads of Roman oppressors perched on the ends of pikes and Jesus barked orders and tactical movements to overthrow the physical system and bondage. He spoke to a deeper, truer bondage, of shackles that clung tighter than their physical oppressors. The chains Jesus spoke of held back the heart of humanity rather than individual freedoms. He gave a series of snapshots of what the attributes of a citizen of God's kingdom actually looked like, known to history as the Beatitudes.

He started each statement with the word "blessed." The definition of "blessed," as Jesus used it, is not what we think about when we think of "blessed." In our culture, we have reduced this word down to a trite expression of delight when things go our way. Blessed here has a deeper connotation. It refers to an inner satisfaction and happiness that does not depend on outward circumstances. The idea here is the world could be falling apart around oneself, but there is an inward, unshakeable satisfaction in the midst of the conflict and turmoil. In Jesus' mind, one could be blessed while every earthly freedom and joy had been stripped away.

With this meaning of blessed in mind, Jesus said, "Blessed are those who are poor in spirit" (Matthew 5:3). Or put another way, blessed are the spiritually bankrupt. Or in other words still, satisfied are those who, when they take stock of all the things they bring to the bargaining table with God, realize they have nothing. The only currency we have in our pockets is our sin and maybe some lint.

Jesus continues this thought in his next "blessed" statement. "Blessed are those who mourn, for they shall be comforted" (Matthew 5:4). Blessed are those who have realized they bring nothing to the table except their sin and mourn, weep, and repent. The kingdom does not go to the people whose plastic religion is smothered in platitudes and self-justification. There is no pulling oneself up by sheer willpower and the American dream in God's kingdom. It goes to the broken and contrite, to the ones who realize we have been separated from God from the very beginning. It is through His mercy alone we can even begin to take part in a story called redemption.

Jesus continued with another blessed statement: "Blessed are the meek, for they shall inherit the earth" (Matthew 5:5). In the United States, we do not like the word "meek." Our picture of "meek" is passive. It lets things slip past. There are no John Waynes rolling into town shooting the bad guys in the word "meek." Something we often miss with this word is it does not mean passive. It is not a doormat. It does not even stay on the sidelines and say nothing. Meek here is better defined as "power under control." A comparable illustration is of a wild stallion who has been caught, bridled, saddled, and broken. It is powerful, but it is submitted

167

to the whims of its master. We do not like the idea of someone "owning us." We are the land of the free. We pride ourselves, because we can do what we want, when we want. Yet Christ calls us His servants (1 Peter 2:16). He calls us to crucify our will to submit to His (Romans 12:1-2). There is no other option.

Jesus followed this statement with, "Blessed are those who hunger and thirst for righteousness, for they shall be satisfied" (Matthew. 5:6). Hunger in this sense is not a craving for a snack in the middle of the day. In Jesus' day, hunger was a real issue. People often did not have enough to eat. The pains of hunger most likely tugged at the sides of many of those who listened to Jesus during this sermon. And our Lord says the kingdom is not for those who hunger for power, food, control, or country; it is for those whose deepest desires are for the righteousness of God—a deeper relationship with God. I find it disheartening how many Christians I come across can rattle off their American rights with dogged intensity and will get caught up in social media arguments or picket in the streets, but be passive when it comes to chasing after Jesus in prayer or studying Scripture. John Piper once said in a tweet, "I am astonished at people who say they believe in God, but live as if happiness is found by giving Him 2% of their attention."[17] In all our striving, Jesus is confronting us with the probing question of where our deepest longings lie.

At times our political activism, our desperate need to be right on social media, and our lobbying for our preferred political party to be in control point to a warped idolatry masquerading as Christianity, no matter how holy we may seem in our motives. This is not to say that political activism is a bad thing—or that God does not care about the humanitarian efforts and causes that have gone on in our world. Christians are called to be where the marginalized and downtrodden are. To be a citizen of God's kingdom is to love as God loves. Political activism not submitted first to the kingdom of God ends in twisted versions of idolatrous Christianity.

The next several statements Jesus made had to do with our conduct. "Blessed are the merciful, for they shall receive mercy. Blessed are the pure in heart, for they shall see God. Blessed are the peacemakers, for they shall be called sons of God" (Matthew 5:7-9). The kingdom does not go to those who are obsessed with power, straining to get ahead at the expense of other people. It goes to the merciful, the peacemaker, and those who are not blinded by their sin. As Jesus was speaking, there was a group of people in the audience known as the Zealots. They were religious radicals who were convinced that in order to regain the sense of kingdom they craved, they needed to use violence to reclaim what the Romans had stolen from them. In fact, in the coming years, they would go on to produce many different rebellions, poking the bear of the Roman Empire long after Jesus' death and resurrection. It would last until AD 70, when Rome had enough and fully invaded Jerusalem and destroyed the temple, squashing the rebellion.

Jesus said violence is not how the kingdom is going to spread. It will not be a kingdom defined by rebellion but founded and grown through love. We show mercy, even to the vilest enemy. A few verses later, Jesus said, "You have heard that it was said, 'You shall love your neighbor and hate your enemy.' But I say to you, Love your enemies and pray for those who persecute you, so that you may be sons of your Father who is heaven" (Matthew 5:43-45). The kingdom Jesus proclaimed is not a longing for the destruction of enemies; it is a hope for their betterment.

Jesus closed out the blessed statements with this:

> *"Blessed are those who are persecuted for righteousness sake, for theirs is the kingdom of heaven. Blessed are you when others revile you and persecute you and utter all kinds of evil against you falsely on my account. Rejoice and be glad, for your reward is great in heaven, for so they persecuted the prophets who were before you." (Matthew 5:10-12)*

We do not like the idea of persecution in America. Growing up, I remember whenever a certain political party would get in office, people worried about sudden persecution. There would be rhetoric of conspiracies about chips to be inserted in the back of hands or foreheads, and that we would not be able to buy or sell without them.

There may be a day when Christianity is no longer tolerated anywhere. In some parts of the world, it has already happened. There are many believers in China and the Middle East who are persecuted on a daily basis because of their faith in Jesus. There may be a day in the United States where the same will happen here. Persecution is a difficult thing. Historically speaking, persecution is the cause of the greatest growth in the Church. It causes people to grow close to Christ and live their faith more boldly—not less. Persecution often brings revival.

Something important to note about persecution in the above passage is it has a prerequisite on it: "for righteousness sake." Jesus said, blessed is your persecution when you encounter resistance because of the righteousness you profess, not for being a jerk. There are churches known for picketing and vandalizing abortion clinics, then claiming persecution when they encounter cultural backlash. Standing for the truth is not an excuse to be a jerk. I have known many Christians who post vulgar images of political candidates they did not like in the name of "speaking truth," only to cry persecution when social media removes it. Resorting to the same smear campaigns the world employs should not be common among believers. The Apostle Peter puts it this way:

> *But even if you should suffer for what is right, you are blessed. 'Do not fear what they fear; do not be shaken.' But in your hearts sanctify Christ as Lord. Always be prepared to give a defense to everyone who asks you the reason for the hope that is in you. But respond with gentleness and respect, keeping a clear conscience, so that those who slander you may be put to shame by your good behavior in Christ. For it is better, if it is God's will, to suffer for doing good than for doing evil. (1 Peter 3:14-17)*

Peter said if someone persecutes you, let it be because you were doing what was right—not for taking part in the same worldly acts the world is doing. When your faith is challenged in the public square, be prepared to give a defense, but it must be done in respect and gentleness. He said to let the only way your persecutors be put to shame not to be by your verbal beatdown, but by the consistent, godly character coming from your life. When Stephen stood before the Sanhedrin in the book of Acts, he was stoned, not for his verbal smackdown, and not for his posting of smear campaigns against other people. His godly character convicted the world around him; they could not stand to be in its presence (Acts 7:54-60).

Jesus also said in this passage, "When you are persecuted." He does not say *if*, He says *when*. Whether on a governmental or personal level—persecution is going to happen. Let it happen because of our righteousness and love, not because we have stooped to the same tactics of the world. However, we aren't necessarily called to be doormats for Jesus. When the soldiers were going to flog Paul in Acts 22, he was quick to remind them that he was a Roman citizen, which stated he could not be beaten without a hearing. The Romans realized they were bound by their own law and did not beat him. Knowing your rights is not wrong. But it must be done in gentleness and respect.

Jesus' outline of a citizen of the eternal kingdom then, it seems, looks much different than the Christian who finds his identity in his country. Our first allegiance is not to country or to a political document or ideals, but rather it is devoted to the gospel and God's kingdom. In another book, Paul wrote, "No soldier gets entangled in civilian pursuits, since his aim is to please the one who enlisted him" (2 Timothy 2:4). The citizen of God's kingdom is first and foremost devoted to Him who enlisted him. He is not a rebel who clings to his rights as a citizen of his earthly nation first and foremost. It is not a brawler who takes his fate into his own hands to take what he feels belongs to himself —rather he "entrusts his soul to a faithful Creator while doing good" (1 Peter 4:19). His chief concern is not personal liberty chasing the pursuit of happiness, but the pursuit of loving God and loving his neighbor as himself.

Just like the people Jesus spoke to on the mountainside, He calls to all of us. He commissions us to be activists not of men's political agendas, but of His Father's agenda. In fact, He calls us His ambassadors. "In Christ God was reconciling the world to himself, not counting their trespasses against them, and entrusting to us the message of reconciliation. Therefore, we are ambassadors for Christ, God making his appeal through us" (1 Corinthians 5:19-20). If you are a believer in Jesus, your chief identifier is no longer American, Jamaican, Russian, Bosnian, or Irish; you are a citizen of the kingdom of God.

As citizens of this kingdom, Christ beckons us to step into the role of being an ambassador to it. We are not called as corny salesman trying to get people into Heaven, but embodying the transforming, burgeoning life of the gospel. He calls us to be the first fruits of God's kingdom on earth. In the seasons at the office where there is discord, He calls us to sow peace. In the times where people weep over personal or national level pain, we are there to empathize and weep with them too. And in the times of persecution, to hold tight to God's promises of the coming kingdom. As citizens of the kingdom of God, He calls us to embody His kingdom on earth, not only in the sweet by and by, but in the here and now.

THE GARDEN

We started our journey together in a graveyard, because most of us think we will carry our deepest issues with us to our grave, despite our desire to change. However, we have talked about how God not only desires for us to change, but His will for our lives is to be day by day transformed into His image. This does not mean it is always simple. It does not mean our knots will necessarily be untied and untangled once we say, "Amen."

I think we often have an unrealistic expectation that our core issues will fall away quickly. Often reality is much different. There is a message in much of our Christian music today, which expresses that our struggles end when the last note of the song resolves. Many of the songwriters will talk about a struggle or sin issue they struggle with, but, by the end of the melody, it has been handled and the singer is basking in the comfort of a clean heart. The truth is, however, for most of us, the struggle wages on. Untangling the knots of our core issues and sanctifying takes cultivation. In fact, becoming more like Jesus is often more like cultivating a garden than laying something to rest in a graveyard. We are not grave keepers watching headstones that will never change; we are gardeners, working in the soil of our lives.

When I was a kid, my parents had a garden. In the early spring, you could find my dad with our old, rickety rototiller wrestling the machine through the soil as he prepared the ground to plant. My mom would then come through with seeds, filling rows with different types of vegetables: a few rows of corn and tomatoes, squash, cucumbers, peppers, and beans, along with others. They would spend hours in the evening bending to pull weeds from in-between the infantile plants and placing sprinklers at strategic points to make sure the whole garden was properly watered. Sometimes, all the work they put into the garden did not seem to be going anywhere. For months, at the end of the day, there was still no fruit on the vine. Nevertheless, year after year, in harvest season, the plants would bend under the weight of its fruit.

As I grew, my parents taught my brother and I to keep the garden. We also would wrestle the rototiller, snap the weeds, and set up the sprinklers to make sure the plants received water during dry parts of summer. I hated weeding the garden. The dirt was hot and would stick in the crevasses between my fingernails. I am sure I complained plenty about it being too hot outside. Yet, year after year, there would come a day where, instead of heading back to the house empty-handed, sweaty, and covered in dirt, I would carry arms full of vegetables into the house.

I think unknotting our sin nature is much the same. It is not instantaneous. We do not often walk into the garden of our heart to till the soil, plant, weed, water, and bring home fruit in the same day. Untangling our knotted hearts is a painful process of repentance, trusting in the promises of God and who He says we are one day, only to find ourselves being dragged kicking and screaming back to desiring the approval of other people or trying to earn God's love. So we repent again. We get back up and keep walking, only to fall down again.

Paul talks about this cycle of sin and repentance in the book of Romans.

For I do not understand my own actions. For I do not do what I want, but I do the very thing I hate.... For I know that nothing good dwells in me, that is, in my flesh. For I have the desire to do what is right, but not the ability to carry it out. For I do not do the good I want, but the evil I do not want is what I keep on doing.... Wretched man that I am! Who will deliver me from this body of death? (7:15-24)

Maybe you can identify with Paul here. Maybe you can identify with the desire to do what is right, but the feeling like the struggle is never-ending.

Our sin is ruthless. We often think we have it eradicated and extricated from our lives, only to find it hiding in some dark corner we had forgotten to check. And if we are not careful, it can regain its stranglehold on our life. I once had a professor in college grimly say to the class, "You must kill your sin, or it will slit your throat." I think the Apostle Paul here would agree.

Our sin does not want to be killed. It desperately strives to retain a claim to the throne of our life. Sometimes, our sin issues shoot up like weeds in the garden of our life. Like Paul, sometimes it can feel impossible to break free of the sin and repentance struggle. Sometimes, working through our core issues takes longer than we think. Sometimes we weed the garden and return the next day to find new ones choking out our tomato plants.

In these moments, in the midst of the struggle, we must return to the gospel and bask in the truth there. In another of Paul's letters, he talks about all of his accomplishments in his life before he met Christ. In the Jewish religious system, Paul would have been considered a superstar. He was circumcised on the eighth day, he followed all the rules, he was the top of the pack. But he says, "But whatever gain I had, I counted as loss for the sake of Christ. Indeed, I count everything as loss because of surpassing worth of knowing Christ Jesus my Lord" (Philippians 3:7-8). No matter what level of goodness he brought to the table, it was not enough. Paul realized he needed God's grace on his best day as much as on his worst day.

The beauty of the gospel is God's grace extends to us on our best and our worst days. Even on the days when the weeds are choking out our gardens. Even when your temptations bang at the door and you feel yourself starting to crack under the pressure. God's grace reaches us even in those places in our lives. As the prophet Jeremiah writes, "The steadfast love of the Lord never ceases; his mercies never come to an end; they are new every morning" (Lamentations 3:22-23). In those moments, when tending to the garden of your life, when the weeds continually return, keep going. Keep tilling the soil.

Paul continued in the letter to the Philippians. After he wrote about counting all of his works as garbage compared to knowing Christ, he shared about continually pressing in to seek after Christ to be found in him not having a righteousness he had earned, but Christ's covering him through faith (Philippians 3:9). He knew chasing after Christ was not going to be without its challenges, and he counted the cost and found it worth it. He concluded:

> *Not that I have already obtained this or am already*
> *perfect, but I person to make it my own, because*
> *Christ Jesus has made me his own. Brothers, I do*

> *not consider that I have made it my own. But one*
> *thing I do: forgetting what lies behind and strain-*
> *ing forward to what lies ahead, I press on toward*
> *the goal for the prize of the upward call of God in*
> *Christ Jesus. (Philippians 3:12-14)*

In the midst of the journey, Paul knew there would be days he would succeed and others when he would fail. When either happened, he decided he would not dwell there. Rather, he would press on. Day after day, he decided to get on his knees, toil in the garden of his life, seeking the fruit Christ was sprouting in him. He was able to do this not because of the effort he exerted in himself; it was because Christ had made him His own.

If you are reading this and you are a believer in Jesus, you are Christ's too. Untangling knots is not easy. Breaking the strongholds of needing the approval of other people, or finding our identity in our country rather than in our Savior, or the myriad other knots that tangle up our lives, can be grueling. But they can be defeated through Christ, through resting in God's promises and basking in the gospel.

C.S. Lewis once shared:

> *Imagine yourself as a living house. God comes in to*
> *rebuild that house. At first, perhaps, you can un-*
> *derstand what He is doing. He is getting the drains*
> *right and stopping the leaks in the roof and so on;*

*you knew that those jobs needed doing and so you
are not surprised. But presently He starts knocking
the house about in a way that hurts so abomina-
bly and does not seem to make any sense. What
on earth is He up to? The explanation is that He is
building quite a different house from the one you
thought of—throwing out a new wing here, putting
on an extra floor there, running up towers, making
courtyards. You thought you were being made into
a decent little cottage: but He is building a palace.
He intends to come and live in it Himself.*[18]

Christ Himself is at work in our lives, making us into
who He has called us to be.

While we are called to garden our lives, to not grow
weary in the midst of the work of sanctification, we must
remember the Master Gardener is working. His promise to us is this: He will complete the work He is creating within us. He will not stop until we look like Him.
Moment by moment, day by day, weed by weed, knot
by knot, God will change us.

BIBLIOGRAPHY

Bonhoeffer, Dietrich, Daniel W. Bloesch, Geffrey B. Kelly, and Victoria Barnett. *Life Together*. Minneapolis, MN: Fortress Press, 2015.

Gaiman, Neil, and Chris Riddell. *The Graveyard Book*. London: Bloomsbury Publ, 2008.

Greear, J. D. *Gaining by Losing: Why the Future Belongs to Churches That Send*. Grand Rapids, MI: Zondervan, 2017.

Greear, J. D., and Spence Shelton. *Gospel: Recovering the Power of Christianity*. Nashville, TN: B & H Publishing Group, 2011.

The Holy Bible: English Standard Version (Wheaton, IL: Crossway Bibles, 2016).

Homer. Rieu, E. V. *The Odyssey*. Baltimore, MD: Penguin Books, 1965.

Horton, Michael Scott. *Ordinary: Sustaining Faith in a Radical, Restless World*. Grand Rapids, MI: Zondervan, 2014.

Keller, Timothy. *Counterfeit Gods: The Empty Promises of Money, Sex, and Power, and the Only Hope That Matters*. New York, NY: Riverhead Books, 2011.

Lewis, C S. *A Grief Observed*. New York, NY: Harper-One, 2015.

Lewis, C. S., and Pauline Baynes. *The Last Battle*. New York, NY: HarperCollins, 1994.

Lewis, C.S. *Mere Christianity/Screwtape*. New York, NY: HarperOne, 2001.

Lewis, C. S. *The Weight of Glory*. New York, NY: Harper-Collins, 2001.

Piper, John. Twitter Post. Mar. 21, 2015, 9:01 AM. https://twitter.com/johnpiper/status/579266627025432576?lang=en

Seuss. *Oh, the Places You Will Go*. New York, NY: Random House, 1990.

ENDNOTES

1. C.S. Lewis, *Mere Christianity/Screwtape*. (New York, NY: HarperOne, 2001), 216.

2. Dietrich Bonhoeffer et al., *Life Together* (Minneapolis, MN: Fortress Press, 2015), 8.

3. J. D. Greear, *Gaining by Losing: Why the Future Belongs to Churches That Send* (Grand Rapids,MI: Zondervan, 2017), 59.

4. C.S. Lewis, *Mere Christianity/Screwtape*. (New York, NY: HarperOne, 2001), 200-201.

5. Neil Gaiman and Chris Riddell, *The Graveyard Book* (London: Bloomsbury Publ, 2008).

6. Homer. Rieu, E. V. *The Odyssey* (New York, NY: Penguin Books, 1965), 190.

7. Ibid, 194.

8. C. S. Lewis, *The Weight of Glory* (New York, NY: HarperCollins, 2001), 26.

9. C S Lewis, *A Grief Observed* (New York, NY: HarperOne, 2015), 9.

10. C. S. Lewis and Pauline Baynes, *The Last Battle* (New York, NY: HarperCollins, 1994), 171.

11. Dietrich Bonhoeffer et al., *Life Together* (Minneapolis, MN: Fortress Press, 2015), 23.

12. Timothy Keller, *Counterfeit Gods: The Empty Promises of Money, Sex, and Power, and the Only Hope That Matters* (New York, NY: Riverhead Books, 2011), xix-xx.

13. J. D. Greear and Spence Shelton, *Gospel: Recovering the Power of Christianity* (Nashville, TN: B & H Publishing Group, 2011), 40.

14. Seuss, *Oh, the Places You Will Go* (New York, NY: 1990), 52, 54.

15. Michael Scott Horton, *Ordinary: Sustaining Faith in a Radical, Restless World* (Grand Rapids, MI: Zondervan, 2014), 89.

16. C.S. Lewis, *Mere Christianity/Screwtape.* (New York, NY: HarperOne, 2001), 227.

17. John Piper. Twitter Post. Mar. 21, 2015, 9:01 AM. https://twitter.com/johnpiper/status/579266627025432576?lang=en.

18. C.S. Lewis, *Mere Christianity/Screwtape.* (New York, NY: HarperOne, 2001), 05.

A C K N O W L E D G M E N T S

I would first like to thank my wife, Amanda, who graciously let me take the time it took to craft this book across all its drafts. Also, I would like to thank her for reading, critiquing, and believing in all of those drafts. Truly, this book wouldn't exist without her.

Nick Westra and Peter Relph deserve a thousand rounds of applause for taking the time to do the painstaking work of reading the first draft and critiquing the work—their critiques added so much to this project.

I would like to thank Edward Cyzewski for his work doing the developmental and copy editing of the book. Also, I have endless praise for Trinity McFadden for her final proofreading of the book. She made it shine.

I have endless thanks Christian Rafetto as well for all his work. He designed the most gorgeous cover for this project; it exceeded all my expectations. He also is responsible for the interior layout of both the paperback and ebook versions of this book.

I am thankful for Humble Books for their part in publishing this book and believing in this project. They have been a pleasure to work with and serve alongside.

Of course, this book would not have been penned if it were not for my loving parents who have supported my love of writing ever since I was a child. Their love of stories transferred to my brother and me; I am forever indebted to them. I would like to thank my Grandma Andringa, who would have loved to see this book but passed away a few years ago. She always asked for chapters of the novels and short stories I was working on when I was in high school. She was my first "fan."

I would like to thank Tiago and Olivia Andrade and the entire team at Mezzo Coffee House. I wrote most of this book there.

Finally, I would like to thank my Lord and Savior Jesus who has been so patient with me in this process. He has been a comforter, an encourager, and an advocate in this process. He has given grace upon grace.

Davis Moore is an author and pastor who resides in West Michigan. Davis synthesizes his roles as an author and pastor, bridging the gap between literature and spirituality. Whether through his sermons or his books, he spreads messages of hope, love, and joy, urging individuals to embrace God's story in their life and find solace in Christ

Davis was born in a small town in West Michigan. He received a love for storytelling from his parents who both relentlessly told him and his brother stories throughout their childhood.

Currently, he is the lead teaching pastor at Corner Bible Church in Allegan, Michigan, where he has served for the last six years. Davis is a storyteller from the stage, passionately communicating the gospel to his congregation. Davis's passion is for people to encounter the identity changing nature of the gospel and helping people live that identity out in their daily lives.

Davis married his high school sweetheart, Amanda. Currently, they live in Allegan, Michigan, with their dog, Nala.

Some of Davis's favorite things are cold brew coffee, sushi, and exploring Michigan's coastal towns with his wife.

www.davismooreauthor.com

humble books

www.humblebooksmedia.com